Wild Flowers
of Malawi

Wild Flowers of Malawi

AUDREY MORIARTY

PURNELL

CAPE TOWN · JOHANNESBURG · LONDON

PUBLISHED IN SOUTH AFRICA BY PURNELL AND SONS (S.A.) (PTY) LTD, 70 KEEROM STREET, CAPE TOWN.

© A. W. MORIARTY 1975

SBN 360 00174 2

LITHOGRAPHIC POSITIVES BY PHOTO SEPRO (PTY) LTD, CAPE TOWN
PRINTED BY ABC PRESS (PTY) LTD, CAPE TOWN
BOUND BY E. D. SEABROOK, CAPE TOWN

FOREWORD
by
SIR PETER WATKIN WILLIAMS
former Chief Justice of Malawi

It gives me the greatest pleasure to respond to Mrs Moriarty's invitation to write a foreword to her book on the flora of Malawi though I must confess that I have no real qualification to do so other than that I was in at the beginning. My wife and I saw the idea form in her mind and then take shape. Now after seven years of hard work it has blossomed like the flowers of which she writes. Malawi is a country of splendid and varied scenery; of high mountains and plateaux, cool by day and frosty by night and, by contrast, of lakes and rivers which swelter in tropical heat. Over much of the country there is a reasonably consistent rainfall and the vegetation is lush, green and fruitful. It is small wonder then that it has a rich and varied flora.

When my wife and I went to live in Blantyre in 1967 we were delighted to find so many beautiful wild flowers in the vicinity, above all the terrestrial orchids, and my wife set to work endeavouring to indentify them. Books of reference of the South African and East African flora were helpful but a number of species appeared to be endemic to Malawi and were not mentioned in these books. Mr E. A. Banda of the Chancellor College Herbarium was most helpful but he was not able to supply information in those cases in which plants had not previously been collected.

Mrs Moriarty was as keen as my wife and they began to work together, the husbands finding themselves abandoned while their wives made trips into the countryside collecting plants. We all went together on holiday to the Nyika Plateau, we climbed Mulanje Mountain, and frequent visits were made to Zomba Plateau. Mulanje Mountain and Zomba Plateau are of the greatest beauty and highly productive of wild flowers but the alpine meadows and dambos of the Nyika Plateau are unsurpassed. Never will I forget the marvellous variety of flowers in the pastures on each side of the Chelinda River at Christmas time where Eulophias, Satyriums and Disa in profusion mingled with Gladiolus, Kniphofias and a host of other plants. Nor will I forget at Easter time the great vistas of *Delphinium leroyi* and *Delphinium dasycaulon*, producing in one place, a superb hybrid of the two, possessing the merits of both.

Owing to the difficulties of identification it became necessary not only to make extensive field notes and to press specimens but to make paintings of each species as well and it then became apparent to us that Mrs Moriarty had a rare talent as a flower artist; a talent which increased with every painting she made. Gradually the idea of writing a book on the flora of Malawi took root in her mind with, I am glad to think, a little pressure on our part and once it had done so, she set about the task with great energy and dedication.

We left Malawi early in 1970 and we were delighted to hear recently that although Mrs Moriarty is no longer resident in Malawi she has been able to complete the work.

I have not been able to see more than a specimen plate of her illustrations at this stage but that is enough to enable me to know that not only has Mrs Moriarty made a most valuable contribution to the bibliography of Malawi but she has supplied a long felt want not only for botanists but for all those who love the countryside and wish to be able to identify what they find in it. In so doing she has undoubtedly produced a work of much charm and beauty.

I am sure that all those into whose hands this book may come will experience the same pleasure as I shall in exploring its pages.

Peter Watkin Williams,
Devon,
England.

Author's Note

When I started to paint the flowers of Malawi I soon realized that for identification purposes I had also to collect and press these flowers. This I did giving each one a collector's number, keeping one specimen for myself and giving the duplicates to the Chancellor College Herbarium in Blantyre. These numbers follow the names of the flowers in the text. Where only one specimen was collected I kept it and so it had no number and these I sent, with my collection, to the Herbarium, at the Royal Botanic Gardens, Kew, England where they are held as Voucher specimens.

I am deeply grateful to Dr R. K. Brummitt of Kew who not only read my very non-technical text and helped me to sort out many problems but also, with his colleagues, checked and identified all the specimens I sent him. Without his help I could not have completed this book.

I also wish to express my gratitude to the Society of Malawi and to The Beit Trust for their generosity in making publication financially possible and to Mr G. D. Hayes for all his help.

To Sir Peter Watkin Williams for so kindly writing a Foreword and who, with his wife Jane, first gave me the urge to turn my paintings into a book.

To Mr A. E. Banda for his helpfulness and in allowing me the use of the Chancellor College Herbarium.

To all my friends in Malawi who came on flower hunting trips, collected plants from mountain peaks beyond my ability to climb, brought me specimens and generally gave me help and encouragement.

And above all to my long suffering husband for his patience and help during the seven and a half years it has taken to produce this book.

To all these I say 'Thank you'.

A. W. Moriarty
George C.P.
South Africa.

CONTENTS

Foreword	v
Author's Note	vii
Families (Refer Index)	1
Botanical Terms	161
Index	163

Plate 1   Araceae

Gonotopus boivinii (Decne.) Engl. (751)

A curious plant up to 90 cm tall. Several compound, bipinnate leaves grow at the top of the fleshy stem, which has snake-like markings at the base. Two or three flowers appear on separate stalks near to the leaf. The spadix, or flower stem, is dull yellow with a swelling at the base. The spathe is a greenish yellow with faint brown and pinkish lines. The plant grows from a thick, round and flattened tuber. It is found at Lujeri, Nasawa and Blantyre at the edge of forests and in rocky scrub.

Flowers November and December.

Plate 1   Araceae

Plate 2   *Amaryllidaceae*

Plate 2   Amaryllidaceae

Crinum pedicellatum Pax   (712)

These large bulbous plants are usually found in moist ground where, if undisturbed and allowed to multiply, they are a magnificent sight at the beginning of the rains. The trumpet shaped flowers have a very long perianth tube which opens into six lobes which are pure white or striped with pink. There are twelve to fifteen flowers at the top of a thick stem which curves upwards from the base of the leaves. The leaves are strap-shaped and up to 150 cm long with undulating edges and very fine hair-like teeth. The lower leaves are spread out on the ground covering a large area. The plants are about 45 cm high. They are found in the Blantyre, Zomba and Mulanje districts.

Flowers November and December.

Plate 3   Amaryllidaceae

Haemanthus multiflorus Martyn (396)

This is a striking perennial which grows from a fairly large bulb. The leaves, which persist long after the flowers are dead, are broad with wavy edges. They and the separate flower stalk appear together from the same sheath each having one flattened side. The large scarlet 'ball' is made up of numerous six-petalled flowers which in turn have long red stamens making the inflorescence even larger, up to 14 cm across. The flowers are borne in an umbel with long papery bracts at the base. These plants are found growing over most of Malawi in grassland and light woodland during the rainy season.
Flowers November to January.

Plate 3 Amaryllidaceae

Plate 4   *Amaryllidaceae   Hypoxidaceae*

Plate 4 Amaryllidaceae

Fig. 1 **Cyrtanthus breviflorus** Harv. (4)

A charming small plant about 12 cm tall with two to four bright yellow flowers in a terminal umbel. The leaves usually appear after, but occasionally with, the flowers. These were found in marshy ground on Nyika Plateau after firing where they glowed through the blackened earth. It is also found on Zomba Plateau.

Flowers July to October.

Fig. 2. **Cyrtanthus welwitschii** Hiern ex Bak. (550)

Also growing in marshy ground, the tubular flowers are a lovely flame colour. The leaves are long, narrow and shiny. It is found on Luchenya Plateau on Mulanje and on Mt Malosa.

Flowers October.

Fig. 3. **Boophone sp.** (683)

A beautiful plant only about 15 cm tall with an inflorescence 7-12 cm across. The individual flowers are pale pink turning to old rose as they mature. They are very fragrant. The umbel has two maroon bracts. The leaves fan out from a long narrow bulb which grows deep in the ground. It is possible that this plant grows only on the open hillsides of the Nyika Plateau where it is locally common. This species has been mistaken for the much more common *B. disticha* but the latter is a far larger plant with the bulb usually only partially buried, the leaves broader and strap-like and the scarlet flowers forming a spherical rather lax inflorescence.

Flowers November and December.

Hypoxidaceae

Fig. 4. **Hypoxis dregei** (Bak.) Nel. (689)

A dainty little plant found growing in baked ground on Mulanje. Only 3-6 cm tall with very narrow leaves and star-like flowers.

Flowers September to June.

Fig. 5. **Hypoxis obtusa** Burch. (205)

This is one of the early spring flowers. The leaves are chanelled, the flower stems flattened, each one bearing several bright yellow flowers which are 2 cm across. The whole plant, including the back of the petals, is covered with fine silvery hairs. It grows from rather a large rootstock and is found on grassy mountain slopes throughout most of Malawi.

Flowers September to December.

Plate 5   Iridaceae

Fig. 1 **Moraea textilis** Bak.   (354)

This lovely autumn flowering Moraea stands 60 cm high on a stem clasped by scale-like leaves with one very long narrow leaf growing from a small corm. The flowers vary from light to deep purple, sepals are spotted at the base, the petals curve up and the stamens are petaloid. It is found growing on dry Brachystgia hillsides on the Nyika Escarpment.

Flowers April and May.

Fig. 2. **Moraea thomsonii** Bak.   (27)

A miniature species, 20-30 cm tall. It appears in baked ground before the rains. There is one brown grass-like leaf. Flowers are pale lilac opening very wide. There are orange markings on the sepals, the stamens are petaloid and divided into two at the tip. Bracts are long narrow and pinkish. As the flowers only open one or two at a time and only from noon for a few hours this attractive little plant can easily be missed. It is found on the Zomba and Nyika Plateaux and Dedza and Mulanje Mountains.

Flowers September to November.

Fig. 3. **Moraea sp.** (Perhaps a variant of *M. schimperi*)

A very graceful plant growing in conspicuous clumps on Luchenya Plateau on Mulanje. There are two to three flowers on a stem. The colour varies from pale mauve to purple. The sepals are narrow and pointed with yellow markings outlined in deep purple. The bracts and stems are pinky brown, so is the ovary which is slender and round. The leaves at the time of flowering are two-thirds the height of the flowering stem which is approximately 45 cm, they are narrowly lanceolate.

Flowers October.

Fig. 4. **Moraea schimperi** (Hochst) Pichi-Sermolli.   (399)

A sturdier species than the previous one with one or two flowers on the stem. Petals and sepals are shorter and more rounded and the corolla tube is wider. The ovary is three-cornered and red in colour, the bracts are long, wide, papery and straw-coloured and encloses the stem. The leaves are long, narrow and lanceolate. It is found on Zomba, Mulanje and Nyika Plateaux and Dedza Mountain.

Flowers September to January.

Plate 5   Iridaceae

Plate 6   *Iridaceae*

Plate 6   Iridaceae

Fig. 1. Crocosmia aurea Planch. (121)

This lovely plant is found at the edge of mountain forests. It is about 60 cm tall. The flower stem is branched and angled bearing many large, bright orange flowers with six flaring petals opening from a long corolla tube. The three stamens and stigma extend well beyond the petals; the leaves are linear and the seeds are most attractive being shiny black in deep red bracts. It is found over most of the high ground of Malawi and is particularly fine on Zomba Plateau.
Flowers February to June.

Fig. 2. Aristea alata Bak. subsp. abyssinica (Pax) H. Weim (447)

Not a very common plant. Two or three buds grow together in a long narrow spathe, they open one at a time and only for a few hours. The flowers are a beautiful deep blue and 2 cm across. The stems are winged, 38 cm tall and the stiff blue-green leaves are about 18 cm. It grows in open grassland and light woodland on Zomba and Mulanje Plateaux.
Flowers February and March.

Fig. 3. Dietes vegeta (L.) N.E.Br. (446)

These fragile white flowers open in the morning and die by noon. The rounded petals are narrow at the base with purple and orange honey guides. They are found in damp shady places in forests and along river edges where the stiff sword-like leaves form a dense ground-cover.
Flowers intermittently throughout the year.

Fig. 4. Moraea angusta Ker-Gawl. (355)

A beautiful plant with one and sometimes two flowers on a stem. They are bright yellow with brown markings on the sepals. The stamens are petaloid and forked, the bracts are brown and do not completely cover the stem. There is one very long grass-like leaf. It is found growing in the dambos by the road south of Kasungu.
Flowers April and May.

Fig. 5. Tritonia laxifolia (Klatt) Benth. ex Bak. (73)

A dainty little plant about 30 cm tall. The flowers are orange to vermillion with a yellow splash and tooth-like process on the three lower petals. Several flowers grow in a one-sided manner on a wiry stem, the lower ones opening first. It is found in open grassland and amongst rocks on Zomba Plateau where it appears to be on the increase. It is also found on Mulanje, Vipya and Dedza Mountains and Chenchere Hill, Chongoni.
Flowers December to April.

Plate 7   *Iridaceae*

Fig. 1. **Anomatheca grandiflora** Bak. (273)

Previously known as *Lapeirousa grandiflora* it has now been reclassified as *Anomatheca*. It is still fairly common but is unfortunately becoming more rare as the rocky hillsides and banks of streams which are its habitat are being cultivated. The beautiful, large clear red flowers have a dark marking on each of the three lower lobes. The corolla tube is very long and slender and the stamens and stigma extend well beyond the corolla lobes. It grows up to 60 cm.

Flowers erratically from January to September.

Fig. 2. **Lapeirousia erythrantha** Bak. (373)

The flowers of this species are very much smaller, usually dark red but occasionally pink, magenta or even white. The stem branches near the top and bears numerous flowers. The leaves are linear with one or two bract-like ones up the stem. Found in grassland under trees along the Michiru road near Blantyre, at Zomba and near Mpatamanga.

Flowers December to February.

Fig. 3. **Radinosiphon leptostachya** (Bak.) N.E.Br. (70)

This dainty little plant grows through tufty grass in rock crevices. The leaves are lanceolate and fan out from the stem which sometimes branches. Flowers are lilac to pink in colour with a dark red stripe on each of the lower three petals. The corolla tube is long and graceful. It is found on Zomba Plateau, Chiradzulu, Dedza district and Nyika.

Flowers January to April.

Fig. 4. **Hesperantha petitiana** (A.Rich.) Bak. var. volkensii (Harms) R. C. Foster (222)

Found growing on dry mountain slopes on the Nyika Plateau and on Mulanje. The stems are maroon, wiry and sometimes branched. The flowers are pink with maroon bracts. The leaves are linear and the plant is about 38 cm high and grows from a small bulb with numerous thread-like roots.

Flowers March to August.

Plate 8   Iridaceae

Plate 8 Iridaceae

Fig. 1. Gladiolus melleri Bak. (702)

One of the first bulbs to appear before the rains. The stem and sheath are maroon, petals scarlet with a crimson glow. The filaments are white. The leaves appear after the flowers. It grows in rocks and grassland on the mountains of Zomba, Sanjika, Dedza, Chongoni and Ntchisi and also on Nyika Plateau where there is a pink variant. It is 60 to 75 cm tall.
Flowers September to February.

Fig. 2. Gladiolus atropurpureus Bak. (366)

A graceful little plant. The white flowers have purple shading on the petals and a purple patch on each of the three lower ones. The filaments are dark with green anthers. The colour varies in this species; this one is found on Zomba Plateau. On Nyambadwe it is much darker, almost purple-black, and on Nyika it is white and pink. All grow on rocky mountain slopes. It is 30 to 45 cm tall.
Flowers November to March.

Fig. 3. Gladiolus erectiflorus Bak. (241)

This delightful plant is found in Brachystegia woodland on the southern end of the Vipya, Dedza district and the Nyika approach. The pale pink petals are heavily veined with red and the stamens are purple. The two or three leaves appear with the flowers and are very narrowly lanceolate. The corm is small and round with a thick root. This is a small species only about 30 cm tall.
Flowers April to June.

Fig. 4. Gladiolus laxiflorus Bak. (72)

A really lovely plant found only in dambos at high altitude. The flowers are a delicate shell pink with a deeper shading in the throat. The three lower petals have a bright yellow splash outlined in dark pink. The anthers are white and the stigma is purple. The flowers open very wide. The plant is about 75 cm tall. It is found on Nyika Plateau.
Flowers October to January.

Fig. 5. Gladiolus natalensis (Ecklon) Reinw. ex Hook.f. (389)

This species, because of the variation in colour has been given many names. It can be found in apricot, orange, scarlet and khaki in different parts of the country. All are strong upright plants with stiff sword-like leaves and all have the upper petal falling forward to form a hood. They are about 90 cm tall. This pure yellow varient is found near the Coronation Dam, Blantyre.
Flowers December to February.

Fig. 6. Gladiolus natalensis (Ecklon) Reinw. ex Hook.f. (604)

A colour form of the same species as Fig. 5. The glorious, large scarlet flowers are streaked with yellow. The sheaths are pinky brown. The flower is hooded but the upper lateral petals fly backwards. The corm is small and very deep with long roots. It is up to 90 cm tall and is found on Ndirande Mountain and Zomba Plateau.
Flowers December to May.

Plate 9 *Iridaceae*

Fig. 1. Gladiolus callianthus Marais. (435)

One of the loveliest of the Iridaceae. It was known as *Acidanthera bicolor* but the genus Acidanthera has now been sunk into Gladiolus. The buds are pale lime green opening to white with dark red markings in the throat. The anthers are purple and the corolla tube is white shaded with pink, 18 cm long and gracefully curved. There are two or three flowers on a stem and these are very fragrant, especially at night. The leaves are linear, one third the length of the stem. This rather rare plant is found growing from a small corm on seepage rocks on Zomba Plateau and also on several hills in the Dedza district.

Flowers December to April.

Fig. 2. Dierama pendulum (L.f.) Bak. (743)

These form large, showy clumps in the grasslands at high altitude. The leaves are long and narrow. The slender stems, up to 120 cm tall, branch near the top, each branch bearing several pendant, pink, bell-like flowers which wave softly in the slightest breeze. The seeds are enclosed in papery bracts. It is found on the Plateaux of Mulanje, Nyika and Vipya.

Flowers most of the year.

Fig. 3. Romulea campanuloides Harms. (00)

Because it is so small this charming little plant is easily overlooked. The flower has six purple petals with maroon stripes on the outer side. The centre is pale green. There are one or two very fine grass-like leaves. The whole plant is only 3-6 cm tall. This one was found on Sombani Plateau, Mulanje in low grass at the edge of a path. It is also found on Zomba, Nyika and Vipya.

Flowers November to April.

Plate 9   Iridaceae

Plate 10   Liliaceae

Plate 10   Liliaceae

Fig. 1. **Gloriosa virescens** Lindl. (374)

A climbing lily which is seen all over Malawi. It is a beautiful plant with many variations in colour, from deep maroon through to flame, giving it its common name of Flame lily. The wavy petals are wider in the centre and curl backwards and inwards. The lower edges and base are yellow. The stamens are very prominent with orange anthers and the stigma is at right angles to the ovary. The leaves are oval with a tendril at the tip with which the plant climbs. Grows at forest edges and in light woodland.

Flowers December to April.

Fig. 2. **Gloriosa superba** L. (448)

Not as common as the last species, it can be recognised by the narrower petals which are very wavy but do not curl inwards like *G. virescens*. The colour is usually all yellow with a little green at the base. They mature to a deep apricot. Both species flower at the same time and can be found in the same places. Height varies considerably from 45 cm to 1-2 metres depending on where it is found.

Flowers December to February.

Plate 11 *Liliaceae*

Fig. 1. **Eucomis undulata** Ait. (106)

A robust green lily which is very common on Zomba Plateau, Nyika, Vipya and on Dedza Mountain. The sturdy stem bears a mass of green flowers above which is a tuft of leaves giving it the common name of Pineapple lily. It is an attractive plant and no less so after the petals have dropped and the calyx and seed capsules remain. These will last in water for several weeks. The leaves are broadly lanceolate with wavy edges. Height is about 30 cm. It grows in grassland and forest margins.
Flowers December to March.

Fig. 2. **Albuca nyikensis** Bak. (351)

A handsome winter flowering plant about 90 cm tall. Flowers are in a fairly dense inflorescence, they are white with a broad green stripe down the centre of each petal. There is a pink papery bract at the axil of each flower stalk. The flowers fade to pinkish brown and the bulb is also pinkish. This one was found on the Kirk range on Matandini Peak. It is also found on Ntchisi and Nyika.
Flowers June to August.

Fig. 3. **Albuca sp.** (161)

Very different is this tiny species. Only 15 cm high with five or six yellowish green flowers and very long, whip-like, cylindrical leaves. It grows in tufts of wiry grass on rocky outcrops on Zomba Plateau.
Flowers March.

Fig. 4. **Androcymbium melanthioides** (359)
Willd var. striatum (Hochst. ex A. Rich.) Bak.

A charming little plant only 3-18 cm tall which is common locally. The large 'petals' are actually modified leaves or bracts, they are white striped with either green or mauve. The tiny flowers nestle in the centre with only the stamens showing. It is found on Ndirande, Zomba, Soche, Dedza and Chongoni mountains.
Flowers November to January.

Fig. 5. **Bulbine abyssinica** A.Rich. (358)

A dainty little bulb with narrow shiny leaves. The stem bears a dense head of bright yellow flowers with very prominent stamens. It grows on rocky hillsides and grasslands over most of Malawi. There is a larger variant than the one illustrated growing on Nyika.
Flowers September to March.

Plate 11   Liliaceae

Plate 12 Liliaceae

23

Plate 12   Liliaceae

Fig. 1. **Dasystachys campanulata** Bak. (460)

A graceful plant up to 1,5 m tall. The inflorescence is densely packed with small white flowers with prominent stamens, the lower flowers opening first. The bracts are dark brown and the leaves long and narrow with slightly wavy edges. These were found growing in damp ground below Ngondola village on Zomba Plateau.

Flowers February to April.

Fig. 2. **Tulbaghia cameronii** Bak. (56)

This is a delightful little plant, 15-25 cm tall. The flowers grow in an umbel subtended by papery bracts. The petals are pink, with the stamens forming a yellow tube in the centre. It is common in the Brachystegia woodlands between Kasungu and Rumphi.

Flowers November to January.

Fig. 3. **Chlorophytum sp.** (563)

This plant is about 20 cm tall. The flowers open at random along the heavy inflorescence. They have white petals and filaments with orange stamens. The bracts are dark brown, and the fruit a three-cornered capsule which forms while the plant is still flowering. The leaves are long and have undulating edges and a deep centre vein. It is found on Zomba Plateau growing in grassland and scrub.

Flowers March to July.

Fig. 4. **Trachyandra saltii** (Bak.) (28)
Oberm. var secunda (Kr. & Dint) Oberm.

One of the first flowers to appear after firing. It has tuberous roots. The old leaves dry out but remain until the following year and from these grow the new cylindrical leaves. The flowers are white with a pink stripe on each petal and the fruit is a round capsule. It is found on grassy hillsides on Zomba Plateau and on Ndirande.

Flowers July to October.

Fig. 5. **Drimia zombensis** Bak. (53)

The stem is about 45 cm tall and maroon in colour. The flowers are in a loose raceme, the petals are greenish and curl backwards over the ovary. Stamens and stigma protrude beyond the petals, they are pink to blue with dark anthers. The leaves appear after the flowers and are linear. It is found on rocky outcrops on Zomba Plateau, Ndirande and on Nyika.

Flowers September to November.

Plate 13 *Liliaceae*

Fig. 1. **Kniphofia grantii** Bak. (684)

The compact, clear yellow flower-heads show up brilliantly above the swamp grasses amongst which they grow. They are up to 40 cm tall, with very long channelled leaves which are a bluish green. The roots form underground stems running horizontally just below the water level. It is found on Nyika Plateau, Vipya, Zomba.

Flowers December to April.

Fig. 2. **Kniphofia** sp. (690)

From 20-60 cm tall, this species grows at high altitude on dry grassy mountain sides. The leaves are not very long, fairly wide and channelled. Flowers are red in bud opening to yellow or sometimes green. The roots are several long cylindrical tubers. They form large splashes of colour on the hilly slopes of the Nyika Plateau.

Flowers December and January.

Fig. 3. **Kniphofia linearifolia** Bak. (413)

This species has a rather untidy inflorescence with buds which open from red to yellow, yellow to green or sometimes all green. It is 60-75 cm tall with very long channelled leaves. The root system in this plant is bulb-like with long tapering roots. It is found on Zomba Plateau in the Mulunguzi Marsh and also on Nyika.

Flowers August to May.

Fig. 4. **Kniphofia splendida** E. A. Bruce (609)

This is a very handsome plant found growing along the Mulunguzi stream on Zomba Plateau and also on Mulanje Mountain. The one illustrated had an inflorescence 25 cm long, the flower stalk and the leaves were each 3 m in length. The buds are a tannish red opening to yellow. The leaves only slightly channelled.

Flowers March to September.

(Flowers on this plate are two-thirds natural size.)

Plate 14   Liliaceae

Plate 14 Liliaceae

These three Aloes are endemic to Malawi.

Fig. 1. **Aloe mawii** Christian (619)

A very spectacular, arborescent species 1-2,5 m high. The stem is up to 12 cm in diam. and branches, each branch bearing a rosette of leaves from which grow one to three flower stalks with the inflorescence carried in a horizontal manner. The flowers point backwards and are sealing-wax red with black protruding filaments and orange stamens. There is also a variant with orange flowers. These aloes are found on the mountains of Mulanje, Ndirande and Chiradzulu and on Zomba Plateau growing on steep, rocky slopes.
Flowers May to July.

Fig. 2. **Aloe mzimbana** Christian (621)

This little aloe is very different from *A. mawii*. It is stemless with broad blue-green leaves which have a bloom and pinky shading, the edges sharply toothed and the sap bright yellow and glutinous. The flower stalk may be single or branched. The flowers are in a dense cylindrical raceme and are pink to red with greenish tips. The stem is reddish brown with a few scaly bracts. It is about 60 cm tall and grows amongst outcrops of rock on Vipya and on Nyika where it is exceptionally fine on Chelinda Hill.
Flowers June to August.

Fig. 3. **Aloe buchananii** Bak. (573)

The leaves of this aloe are long, narrow and channelled with white markings at the base. The flowers are borne at the top of a 45-90 cm stem and vary in colour from salmon pink and green on Ndirande to a much darker shade of red on the Kirk range and on Mulanje Mountain.
Flowers April to June.

(This plate is one-third natural size.)

Plate 15 *Liliaceae*

Fig. 1. **Eriospermum abyssinicum** Bak. (763)

About 20 cm tall, the simple raceme has long pedicels for each yellow flower. The fruit is a capsule containing woolly seeds which are dispersed by the wind. The single leaf is stiff and broadly lanceolate with a long stalk, appearing after the flowers, from a round, flat corm. Occurs on Nyambadwe Hill, Nasawa and Michiru also Zomba and Balaka in shallow soil on outcrops of rock.

Flowers October to December.

Fig. 2. **Dipcadi** sp. (765)

Easily missed, this dainty little lily varies in colour from pale green to white and brown. The flowers are tubular, the three inner 'petals' being broad and flat and the outer ones longer and curled inwards at the tips forming a curious little pocket, and are honey scented. It has long narrow leaves and appears to favour light soil amongst rocks. It is found on Nyambadwe Hill and at Njuli.

Flowers November to January.

Fig. 3. **Scilla cordifolia** Bak. (414)

This tiny plant grows in marshy ground. The two broad leaves are nearly flat on the ground, they are a dark purplish-brown from the centre of which appear one to three stalks about 7-12 cm high. The flowers are in a loose raceme, the petals are green and roll backwards, the filaments are purple and prominent with yellow stamens. Found occasionally on Zomba Plateau and in dambos round Blantyre and Limbe.

Flowers November and December.

Fig. 4. **Scilla rigidifolia** Kunth (695)

A charming little bulb first seen growing in burnt ground on Nyika Plateau, it is also found on Vipya. The flowers are in a cone-shaped head with pale purple petals with a dark purple centre and turquoise stamens. It is 10-15 cm high. The narrow leaves appear after the flowers from a comparatively large bulb.

Flowers October to January.

Plate 15   Liliaceae

Plate 16   Liliaceae

Plate 16 Liliaceae

Fig. 1. **Scilla buchananii** Bak. (381)
This little plant is found frequently in dry grassland. The leaves are shiny and often mottled with purple. Two or three stems curve up from the centre carrying greenish-grey to turquoise flowers with purple stamens. The plant may be from 5-30 cm high depending on conditions.
Flowers December and January.

Fig. 2. **Scilla natalensis** Planch. (677)
One of the most beautiful of the lily family. To see several of these flowers clinging to the rocks overhanging the deep pools of the Chapeluka Gorge, on Mulanje, is a sight not to be forgotten. The exposed bulbs send out a stem which may be 90 cm long and grows in a horizontal manner, it has hundreds of Jacaranda-coloured flowers each on a slender stalk of the same colour. The stamens are yellow. The bulb is scaly with strong roots which hold it on to the rocks. The leaves are maroon below, when young, and shiny green above, and do not appear until after the flowers. It may also be found on moist sloping grassland on Mulanje plateaux.
Flowers October.

Fig. 3. **Wurmbea tenuis** (Hook.f.) Bak. (55)
A tiny plant, 5-8 cm tall, which clusters in moist, rocky depressions. The bulb is small and flat with a single stem which divides and carries one to three terminal flowers. The six petals are white with a dark bar across the base, the anthers are yellow and the filaments mauve. There is one narrow lanceolate leaf with one or two bract-like ones on the stem. It is found on the Nyika Plateau and also on Chongoni Mountain.
Flowers November to January.

Plate 17   Tecophilaeaceae

Fig. 1. **Walleria mackenzii** Kirk (520)

A most attractive plant with light, shiny green, alternate leaves, from the axil of which appears a slender flower-stalk with one small bract half way up and a single terminal flower. The six petals are a beautiful lavender blue with dark blue filaments and yellow anthers. Not very common but it may be found on Chiradzulu and round Ntondwe, Chikala and Kasungu.
Flowers November to January.

Eriocaulaceae

Fig. 2. **Eriocaulon schimperi** Koern. (54)

A plant which grows in very marshy ground. The leaves are light green and channelled forming a basal rosette. The terminal inflorescence is a round knob composed of minute white flowers. The stem may be 10-90 cm tall and is enclosed below in a bract-like leaf. It is probably known only from Nyika in Malawi and is prolific round Lake Kaulime.
Flowers most of the year.

Velloziaceae

Fig. 3. **Xerophyta** sp. (104)

This plant previously known as *Vellozia*, under new classification has been changed to *Xerophyta*, *Vellozia* itself being restricted to South America. The stems of *Xerophyta* are dry, fibrous and branched and may reach 3,5 m in height. The plant looks completely dead until the leaves appear when they cluster at the tips of the stems and are rough and grass-like. The flowers are unexpectedly beautiful; they have six petals which may be white, pink or pale purple, the style is green and the stamens are yellow, the flower-stalk and calyx are green and covered with shiny, sticky globules. It is found on the rocky windswept mountain slopes of Mulanje and Zomba Plateau where the specimen illustrated was collected.
Flowers September to November.

Plate 17 Tecophilaeaceae Eriocaulaceae Velloziaceae

Plate 18   Zingerberaceae

Plate 18 Zingerberaceae

Fig. 1. **Kaempferia aethiopica** (Solms) Benth. (719)
This is a very lovely flower which grows straight out of the ground after the first rains. It is 10 cm tall with three bract-like petals which are yellow and form a tube out of which appear the beautiful purple staminodes. The upper ones are hooded, while the lower one falls forward with two yellow splashes in the throat. The leaves are not seen until after the first flowers have faded but they persist for many months. They are broadly lanceolate and canna-like, a soft green with slightly wavy edges. It is found round Blantyre, Zomba and right through to Vipya and Misuku.
Flowers October to January.

Fig. 2. **Kaempferia rhodesica** Thr.Fr. (720)
A larger flower than the previous one, it is about 15 cm tall. The staminodes are pure white except for a yellow throat, very fragile and looking like tissue paper. The back ones are upright, the front ones fall forward. The leaves are stiff and bluish green, up to 60 cm tall, lasting for long after the flowers. I have only found this species in the Northern Province south of Rumphi, where it grows amongst trees on steep hillsides.
Flowers November and December.

Fig. 3. **Kaempferia rosea** Schweinf. ex Benth. (375)
Unlike the last two species, this one has a flower stem with several flowers opening one or two at a time. They are pale or dark pink with a yellow splash on the lower staminode and a darker marking on either side. The leaves are in a sterile shoot and canna-like. It is found throughout Malawi in light woodland.
Flowers November and December and on until February in the North.

Fig. 4. **Kaempferia decora** Van Druten (376)
Very like the last species but the flowers are a brilliant yellow and are more upright. It is not as common as *K. rosea* but is found on wooded slopes on the Chikwawa road and at Mulanje.
Flowers November and December.

Fig. 5. **Costus spectabilis** (Fenzl) K. Schum. (377)
The flower rises from four furled, grey-green leaves which are edged with maroon. These, as they mature, drop back and lie flat on the ground. Other flowers rise singly from the centre. There is one large, curved, bright yellow staminode which falls forward in front forming a lip and is 12 cm across. It is a very lovely species and is found under trees and on old anthills.
Flowers November and December.

Fig. 6. **Aframomum angustifolium** (Sonn.) K. Schum. (398)
The flowers grow from horizontal underground stems, quite separate from the tall canna-like leaves. There are three pink bracts, and the staminodes are pale pink with yellow markings. It is found in most of the deep rain forests of Malawi.
Flowers October to December.

(Illustrations on this plate are half natural size.)

Plate 19 Commelinaceae

There are many species of this family in Malawi and the colour range is large. They make bright patches in the dry grassland and on the forest edges, but because most of them flower for only a few hours in the morning they are often overlooked.

Fig. 1. **Commelina zambesiaca** C.B. Cl. (363)

One of the larger flowered species. The two fragile petals are a beautiful sky-blue and rise from a folded spathe. The plant is semi-procumbent and is found growing over banks round Zomba and Blantyre and also on Nyika. Flowers January to April in the south and as late as July in the north.

Fig. 2. **Commelina neurophylla** C.B. Cl. (159)

A compact plant growing in the higher grasslands. The two mauve petals are stalked, spathes are dark green above and yellowish below. Leaves sheath the stem. It is found on Zomba Plateau, Chongoni and Nyika.
Flowers January to July.

Fig. 3. **Commelina africana** L. (368)

This has small yellow flowers and is a rather straggling plant. The leaf sheaths are brown and striped. It is found in grass and scrub over most of Malawi.
Flowers December to April.

Fig. 4. **Commelina diffusa** Burm.f. (385)

The small blue flowers appear on stalks from the folded bracts. The leaf sheaths are reddish and hairy. The stems root at the nodes and reach great length. It has become a weed on cultivated lands.
Flower January to May.

Fig. 5. **Commelina aspera** Benth. (518)

Rather a different type as there are several bracts above each other bearing small apricot flowers. The leaves are pointed and striped with maroon, as are the stems. It roots from the nodes and is approximately 20 cm high. It is found on Ndirande and Michiru.
Flowers April.

Fig. 6. **Murdannia simplex** (Vahl) Brenan (364)

A plant up to 60 cm tall. It has long, narrow leaves which sheath the stem and strong hairs near the axil. The stem branches and bears lavender-coloured flowers with three petals. The two filaments are purple and feathery with yellow anthers. The flowers grow in a one-sided manner leaving a scar on the stem when they drop. It is found widespread in grassland, scrub and woods.
Flowers September to April.

Plate 19 Commelinaceae

Plate 20   Commelinaceae

Plate 20 Commelinaceae

Fig. 1. **Floscopa glomerata** (Willd. ex J. A. & J. H. Schult.) Hassk. (102)

An erect herb which grows in shallow water. Leaves are lanceolate and alternate. Flowers are in a crowded inflorescence, mauve with purple bracts, and long curving filaments with yellow anthers. The whole flower-head appears to be covered with tiny glistening hairs. It is found at Chagwa Dam on Zomba Plateau and many localities including Nyika, Vipya and Dedza. Flowers March to October.

Fig. 2 **Cyanotis speciosa** (L.f.) Hassk. (360)

The leaves are lanceolate, alternate. Flower-heads grow from the top of the stem and also from the leaf axil. The numerous, spiky bracts form a cone from which appear the almost invisible flowers with their conspicuous hairy filaments and yellow anthers. They look like small blue powder-puffs. Found in grassland and under trees on high ground. Flowers November to February.

Fig. 3. **Aneilema welwitschii** C.B.Cl. (531)

The tiny flowers are orange with yellow stamens and dark blue stigma. They are arranged in a closely packed, terminal inflorescence. The leaves are long with conspicuous veins and sheath the stem. It is about 24 cm high and is found under trees round Kasungu and Dedza. Flowers December to March.

Fig. 4. **Aneilema hockii** De Wild (406)

About 60 cm tall, the flowers are pale purple with two upper petals which are broad above and narrow below and one lower one which is narrow and curves downwards. There are three boat-shaped bracts which are maroon and shining. Filaments are long and curved. The leaves enfold the stem. It is found round Blantyre, Thyolo, Dedza and Vipya. Flowers December to April.

Fig. 5. **Aneilema aequinoctiale** (Beauv.) Kunth (386)

The flowers are yellow and the small lower petal is rounded. The leaves are covered with sticky hairs, and are purplish brown where they sheath the stem. It is about 60 cm tall and is found over most of Malawi. Flowers all the year round.

Fig. 6. **Cyanotis foecunda** Hassk. (534)

A semi-prostrate plant found at the edge of seepage rocks. The stems are angled at each bract and are covered with fine hairs. The flowers lie in the bracts with white fluffy filaments with orange anthers. The plant is pale green when young, turning maroon as it matures. This one was found at Bembeke. Flowers March.

Fig. 7. **Cyanotis longifolia** Benth. (445)

About 20 cm tall. The bracts are ridged and curved in a one-sided manner with one or two long narrow leaves immediately below. Flowers are inconspicuous but the filaments, which are usually blue but very occasionally pink, are prominent with their orange anthers. Found widespread in grassland and scrub. Flowers December to March.

Plate 21 Orchidaceae

The Eulophias form a large group of the terrestrial orchids of Malawi, and produce some of the most showy and colourful flowers. In all species the lip forms a spur at the back and the leaves are carried on a separate, sterile stem.

Fig. 1. **Eulophia euantha** Schltr. (00)

This grows in sandy Brachystegia woodland. It is about 22 cm. tall with three to six large rather flat flowers at the top of the stem. The sepals and petals are pink, the lip has a deep maroon splash and the spur is short and narrow. The leaves are on a separate stem and appear at the same time as the flowers, they are long and very slender. This is a lovely plant found at Dzalanyama and from Kasungu to Rumphi.
Flowers December and January.

Fig. 2. **Eulophia** sp. (58)

The russet brown sepals and petals are narrow and curve upwards. The spur is short and yellowish, and the lip is long and white with white or pale brown hairs in the centre, the side lobes have faint brown lines. The only leaves seen were two small bract-like ones clasping the base of the stem. They were brown. It is found at Likabula, Mulanje.
Flowers November.

Fig. 3. **Eulophia coeloglossa** Schtr. (39)

A curious orchid, the pink flowers with their stiff shiny green or chocolate-brown sepals, look like small lanterns. The lip is pink to cherry, the spur short and stubby. The plant is about 40 cm tall and grows from a horizontal, underground root in very wet dambos. Found on Nyika and Dzalanyama.
Flowers November to January.

Fig. 4. **Eulophia thomsonii** Rolfe (685)

Found at high altitude, this species has a short stout stem with three or four creamy flowers at the top. The lip has a maroon or almost black splash, but as the flowers do not open wide these are not easily seen. It is about 25 cm high. Found in dry grassland on Nyika Plateau.
Flowers October to January.

Fig. 5. **Eulophia orthoplectra** (Reichb.f.) Summerh. (52)

About the first orchid to appear at the end of the dry season. It is 45-60 cm tall. Sepals are small and brown, petals bright yellow above and dark red or striped with maroon underneath. Spur is short, and narrow at the tip, column is bright green with yellow anther cap. The lip is keeled with yellow ridges. The leaves appear after the flowers. Found on Ndirande, at Thyol and Dedza.
Flowers August to November.

Plate 21   Orchidaceae

42

Plate 22 Orchidaceae

Plate 22 Orchidaceae

Fig. 1. **Eulophia livingstoniana** (Reichb.f.) Schltr. (390)

A graceful plant 30-60 cm high with up to twelve flowers in a loose raceme. The sepals turn back over the ovary and the petals have a minute point at the tip, both being lilac in colour. The lip turns down and is frilled at the lower edge, while the side lobes are semi-circular and green and the keels on the lip are deep purple. The leaves are narrowly lanceolate and appear after the flowers. It is found throughout Malawi in grassland and light woodland.
Flowers September to December.

Fig. 2. **Eulophia zeyheri** Hook.f. (379)

A showy species up to 45 cm tall. There is a short dense spike of large, lemon-yellow rather bell-like flowers each with a deep orange splash on the lip. The leaves appear on a separate stalk at the same time as the flowers, and are broad, sword-shaped and very deeply veined. It is found in grassland and under Brachystegia over most of Malawi.
Flowers October to January.

Fig. 3. **Eulophia paivaeana** (Reichb.f.) Summerh. (378)

This sturdy orchid will grow up to 1,5 m tall in favourable conditions. There are several flowers in a loose raceme. The three sepals are greenish brown, petals a bright yellow with the lip yellow with purple side lobes. The ovary is maroon, and bract green turning straw coloured and papery. The leaves are large, wide and sword-shaped and are heavily pleated, appearing at the same time as the flowers. It grows in sunny grassland and also in deep shade in gum plantations round Blantyre, Mulanje, Dedza and through to Nyika.
Flowers August to January.

Fig. 4. **Eulophia speciosa** (R.Br. ex Lindl.) Bolus (391)

A glowing orchid which stands up to 90 cm tall, well above the grasses in which it grows. The sepals are small, olive green, and turn back along the ovary. The petals and lip are brilliant yellow with a few red streaks on the side lobes of the lip which turns up at the tip. The column is green. It is found over most of Malawi.
Flowers October to February.

Fig. 5. **Eulophia cucullata** (Sw.) Steud. (380)

One of the commonest orchids throughout the country. It is up to 80 cm tall with about six large showy flowers which vary from pale pink to deep purple. The three pointed sepals which are greenish brown, sweep back along the ovary. The lip opens into a sac-like cavity which is spotted with purple. The spur is short and very broad. It grows in grassland and light woodland.
Flowers September to February.

Plate 23 Orchidaceae

Fig. 1. **Eulophia kirkii** Rolfe (766)

This is a very elegant orchid. The three sepals are green and two petals are pure white. The lip is whitish green with purple processes in the centre. The spur is short and curves forward. The plant is about 60 cm tall. The leaves appear after the flowers and are very broad and pleated. It grows under pine forest in Limbe, the lower slopes of Ndirande and on Zomba Plateau.
Flowers December and January.

Fig. 2. **Eulophia complanata** Verdoorn (32)

Found in grassland and on dambo edges on the Nyika Plateau. The sepals are green maturing to brown and inclined to turn backwards. The petals are cream to yellow, the lip with orange markings. There are seven to eight flowers in a loose raceme. It is about 20 cm tall.
Flowers December to February.

Fig. 3. **Eulophia walleri** (Reichb.f.) Kraenzl. (463)

An unusual Eulophia with showy flowers in a loose raceme. The three long narrow sepals are orange to vermillion and are darker than the petals. The lip is spoon-shaped, red with orange processes in the centre. The bracts are long and thread-like. Found in the dambos and in Brachystegia woodlands on the Lake Chilwa road and on the Shire Highlands near Lilongwe and between Mzimba and Livingstonia.
Flowers January to March.

Fig. 4. **Eulophia macrantha** Rolfe (464)

A most beautiful orchid growing up to 90 cm high under bamboo in Limbe and in Zomba. The flowers are large, petals and sepals are a pale primrose-yellow, the lip is dark maroon, almost black with processes right to the tip. The stem is very like the bamboo under which it grows, it is strong and covered with straw-coloured bracts. This orchid is well worth protecting as it is, apparently, of very limited distribution.
Flowers February.

Plate 23   Orchidaceae

Plate 24 Orchidaceae

Plate 24 Orchidaceae

Another large genus of the orchid family are the Disas. These differ from the Eulophias in having the spur formed by the hooded dorsal sepal and not by the lip which is a modified petal. The leaves may be carried on the flowering stem or on a sterile shoot. The plants may be terrestrial or epiphytic on trees or rocks.

Fig. 1. **Disa erubescens** Rendle (33)

One of the loveliest and most spectacular of Malawi's terrestrial orchids, growing at high altitude in dambos. The three or four flowers on a stem are scarlet or orange. The hood is spotted with a short strap-like spur at right angles, while the side sepals spread backwards like wings, and the lip is long and narrow. Some magnificent specimens are found on Nyika where it is common, and some smaller ones on Zomba Plateau where it is rather rare.
Flowers December to March.

Fig. 2. **Disa ornithantha** Schltr. (46)

Not unlike the previous orchid but much smaller. The 'neck' below the hooded sepal is very short. The leaves are bract-like and clasp the stem. It grows in pockets of shallow soil on seepage rocks on Zomba Plateau and on Nyika.
Flowers December to March.

Fig. 3. **Disa saxicola** Schltr. (64)

A dainty little orchid 8–20 cm high found growing in clumps of wiry grass on rocks and in crevasses often with *Radinosiphon leptostacha*. Lateral sepals and petals are white to pale pink, the lip and hooded dorsal sepal have dark red spots, as have the ovaries and stems. The spur is dark red and the leaves narrowly lanceolate, a delicate green, wavy and edged with purple. It is found on Zomba Plateau, Ndirande and possibly other higher rocky peaks.
Flowers January to March.

Fig. 4. **Disa robusta** N.E.Br. (38)

This is a well-named orchid as it is a sturdy plant standing 45 cm high in short dry grass. The flowers are usually orange or vermilion but occasionally yellow or apricot. The hooded sepal has a long erect spur and it is spotted inside. The side sepals are widely spread or fly backwards over the ovary. Ovary and bracts are green spotted with red, and the leaves are bract-like and clasp the stem, the lower ones deeply marked with maroon. A common orchid on Nyika and occasionally found on Zomba Plateau.
Flowers November to January.

Plate 25 Orchidaceae

Fig. 1. **Disa hircicornis** Reichb.f. (41)

A robust plant up to 50 cm high. The leaves are strap-shaped, pointed, and decrease into bracts towards the inflorescence, they are spotted with purple. The flowers are in a dense raceme, and are dark purple to mulberry. The dorsal sepal has a long, narrow spur which turns down at the tip. It is found on the damp ground on Nyika and Zomba Plateau and on Mt. Soche and Dzalanyama.

Flowers January to April.

Fig. 2. **Disa hircicornis** Reichb.f. (42)

This charming Disa with its elegant colouring is also *D. hircicornis* which is a very variable species in both colour and form. The hood is pinkish-grey with dark red margins. The lateral sepals are dark red edged with white, the lip narrow, white and broad at the tip. The leaves are light green and overlap the stem. The height is about 40 cm. It is found on Nyika and Zomba Plateaux, the two forms often growing together.

Flowers December to February.

Fig. 3. **Disa concinna** N.E.Br. (36)

A slender species with an open raceme of white to pale purple flowers. The dorsal sepal forms a tall bonnet-like spur and is spotted in the front, while the lateral sepals face forward. The ovaries and stem are heavily spotted with purple. The leaves are narrow lanceolate and clasp the stem. It is found on Nyika and Zomba Plateaux, on Ndirande, Chongoni and the Kasungu district.

Flowers January to May.

Fig. 4. **Disa hamatopetala** Rendle (37)

A truly beautiful orchid. The large flowers are in a very loose raceme. The spur is blunt and greenish, sepals vary from pale sky blue with pink undertones to deep blue or purple. The lip may be almost white to royal blue and is deeply cut into long slender processes. It stands up to 45 cm tall in high altitude grassland. It is found on Mulamje Mountain, Nyika Plateau and less commonly on Zomba Plateau.

Flowers September to December.

Fig. 5. **Disa Welwitschii** Reichb.f. (43)

This seems to grow equally well in dry grassland and in marshy ground. It is about 35 cm. tall. The flowers are a most glorious crimson, borne in a tight raceme, opening very wide, and with a short pointed spur. The leaves clasp the stem except for one long narrow one which grows from the base. It is common on Nyika and is also found at Kasungu and Mzimba.

Flowers November to February.

Plate 25   Orchidaceae

Plate 26   Orchidaceae

51

Plate 26 Orchidaceae

Habenaria is another terrestrial genus. The flowers are usually green or green and white. The column has two, free, club-shaped stigmata projecting forward like 'eyes'. The lip may be entire or with three lobes which in turn may be deeply divided. The flowers often resemble insects or 'faces'.

Fig. 1. **Habenaria gonatosiphon** Summerh. (35)

Not very common, the only two specimens found each had three flowers branching from the top of a 38 cm stem. This is loosely clasped by bract-like leaves. The dorsal sepal is hooded, the lateral ones like wings. Each upper petal is divided into two narrow horns, while the lip is narrow and white, curving downwards. The spur is 7,5 cm long and tucked into the bracts. It is found in wet grassland and dambos on Nyika Plateau.
Flowers December and January.

Fig. 2. **Habenaria walleri** Reichb.f. (65)

This is a conspicuous orchid about 90 cm tall. The large flowers at the top of the stem are stalked. The dorsal sepal is hooded, lateral sepals curve backward and are green. The petals and trilobed lip are white and flare out in front catching the breeze and dancing above the surrounding grasses. The spur is very long, 18 cm, and widening at the tip. It grows in marshy ground along Lake Chilwa Road and is also found round Blantyre, Dedza and Kasungu.
Flowers December to January.

Fig. 3. **Habenaria tentaculigera** Reichb.f. (419)

An all-green species except for a slight pinkish tinge. The hood is broad with a narrow rim, sepals wing-like and petals very narrow like tentacles from which it gets its name. Found in moist grassy clumps on rocks on Zomba Plateau and round Kasungu.
Flowers December and January.

Fig. 4. **Habenaria macrostele** Summerh. (160)

About 35 cm tall, the leaves are long, lanceolate and clasp the stem. The column is white with yellow anther caps The green sepals are narrow and wing-like while the petals are green and also narrow, the lip is tri-lobed giving a spider-like appearance. It is found on Zomba Plateau.
Flowers January to March.

Fig. 5. **Habenaria pubipetala** Summerh. (477)

The sepals are green. The two upper petals are white and curve inwards. The lip has three lobes the centre one slightly curved and the outer and longer ones curled up like springs. The spur bends backward and is thicker at the tip. It is found on Zomba Plateau and on Mount Soche.
Flowers March.

Fig. 6. **Habenaria** sp.

This is the single flower of a quaint little gnome-like orchid about 35 cm tall. I only found one plant on Dedza Mountain and was unable to get a pressing for identification. It grows like H. pubipetala in mountain grassland.
Flowers March.

Plate 27 Orchidaceae

Fig. 1. **Cynorkis kirkii** Rolfe (416)

A curious little orchid about 22 cm tall, usually with only two to five flowers although I have found them with up to fourteen on a stem. The hood is cream, sepals and petals pink darkening towards the tip. The lip is four-lobed, creamy-yellow with pink tips. The spur is pink, long, narrow and curves forward. It is found in small colonies on wet rocks and mossy hollows on Zomba Plateau and Mt. Soche.
Flowers December to March.

Fig. 2. **Cynorkis kassnerana** Kraenzl. (60)

A lovely orchid which is found growing in large numbers under pine trees on Zomba Plateau, Nyika and Mulanje. The flowers are two shades of purple, the hood being the darkest. The lip is three-lobed and the spur is short and lies along the ovary curling forward at the tip. The stem is maroon to green and is covered with fine hairs There is usually only one shiny basal leaf which is purple underneath.
Flowers March and April.

Fig. **Disperis dicerochila** Summerh. (66)

A charming little plant easily overlooked, found on Zomba Plateau growing on banks of streams and mossy waterlogged trees. From 7-15 cm tall, the stem is purplish-green with a pair of ovate leaves half-way up and a pair of similar bracts below the one to three flowers. These are pink with dark red markings and the side sepals have curious sac-like pouches towards the front.
Flowers February and March.

Fig. 4. **Brachycorythis pleistophylla** Reichb.f. (40)

This is a handsome plant up to 60 cm. The leaves are bract-like and clasp the stem and, like the bracts, are long and very pointed with purple edges and markings. The flowers, in a fairly dense raceme, are lilac and purple with a yellow centre. The two lobes of the lip are boat-shaped and extend forward. It is found in wooded grassland on Zomba and Nyika Plateaux and on Ndirande and Soche Mountain.
Flowers November and December.

Fig. 5. **Stenoglottis fimbriata** Lindl. (67)

This delightful little orchid is found on mossy rocks or trees in rain forests and along streams. There are two or three tuberous roots, and a rosette of pale green lanceolate leaves with wavy edges. The flower stalk is maroon and spotted, the flowers are in a loose raceme. The sepals are brilliant purple, the petals paler, the lip tri-lobed with the centre lobe the longest pale pink with purple spots. The plant is 8-20 cm tall and is found on the mountains of Mulanje, Soche, Dedza, Ndirande and on Zomba Plateau.
Flowers December to June.

Plate 27   Orchidaceae

Plate 28   Orchidaceae

Plate 28   Orchidaceae

Fig. 1. **Bulbophyllum oxypterum** (Lindl.) Reichb.f. (479)

A common epiphyte on trees and rocks in rain forest. Each conical pseudo-bulb bears two shiny green leaves. The flower-stem thickens at the inflorescence and looks like a lobster's claw. It is yellow, mottled with maroon. The small flowers grow alternately up each side and are dark red to purple, and are most attractive when seen through a magnifying glass. They are found on Mulanje, Soche and Ndirande Mountains, at Thyolo and on Zomba Plateau.
Flowers October to February.

Fig. 2. **Polystachya sp** (418)

A delightful little orchid which grows on the edge of windswept rocks in tufts of wiry grass. The flowers have brown sepals, pink petals and a lip which is also pink and turns up at the tip. Only two to five flowers on a stem and two or three shiny leaves growing from the pseudobulbs. It is 4–8 cm tall and is found on Zomba Plateau.
Flowers December to February.

Fig. 3. **Oberonia disticha** (Lam.) Schltr. (00)

A tiny orchid which grows out horizontally from the host tree. The rather fleshy, overlapping leaves have a flattened appearance. The inflorescence is a plume of minute dull orange flowers. The entire plant is no more than 6–8 cm long, slightly smaller than illustrated. It is found in the rain forests at Namgwiri, Bvumbwe.
Flowers February.

Fig. 4. **Schwartzkopffia lastii** (Rolfe) Schltr. (00)

A saprophitic plant the flowers of which appear just above the ground. Petals and sepals are pale purple. The lip is tri-lobed, deep purple with an orange splash. The remainder of the plant is underground, the stem being covered with leaf-like bracts. The plant above and below ground is only about 7 cm high. Found in wooded grassland on Ndirande, Soche and Dedza Mountains and Nyika.
Flowers November to January.

Fig. 5. **Polystachya johnstonii** Rolfe (676)

Epiphytic only on *Xerophyta* (which was known as *Vellozia*). These attractive little flowers appear from clusters of dry-looking pseudo-bulbs. The sepals may be pale pink or mauve, the lip dark red or purple. Two or four flowers form a low posy. The leaves come after the flowers and are green, shiny and edged with purple. This species is found on Mulanje, Zomba Plateau, Ndirande and Chiradzulu.
Flowers September and October.

Plate 29   Orchidaceae

Fig. 1. **Platycoryne crocea** (Schweinf. ex. Rchb.f.) (45)
Rolfe subsp. elegantula (Kraenzl.) Summerh.
  This orchid grows in seepage grassland and is about 30 cm tall. There are two to five flowers at the top of a slender stem. The sepals and petals are narrow and suberect. The spur hangs down and is thickened at the tip. A few bract-like leaves clasp the stem. It is found round Blantyre but is not very common.
Flowers February and March.

Fig. 2. **Platycoryne mediocris** Summerh. (436)
  A cheerful orchid with brilliant orange flowers which are nearly at right angles from the top of the stem. The lip curls down and the spur thickens at the tip. The few leaves clasp the stem. It is found in Brachystegia woodland from Zomba Plateau through Dedza, Kasungu and to the North. Very like it, but found in Blantyre and Lujeri, is *P. buchananiana* Kraenzl. In this species the flowers are larger and the lip turns up and the leaves form a tuft at the bases of the stem.
Flowers December to February.

Fig. 3. **Nervilia** sp. (761)
  The leaves are pointed, ovate and deeply veined with long purple stalks, appearing at the same time as the flowers or just after them. Stems and bracts are brownish-purple. Flowers are greenish-brown with purple tinges. The lip has green side lobes, and the longer centre lobe curves under and has purple stripes. It is not common and is found at the foot of trees in Limbe. It grows to about 15 cm.
Flowers November.

Fig. 4. **Liparis nervosa** (Thunb.) Lindl. (69)
  A curious small orchid with large oval satiny leaves which are deeply veined. It grows from pseudobulbs. The stem is square, about 30 cm. high, and the flowers are in a lax raceme. Sepals and column are green, the lip is two-lobed, convex and deep purplish-red. The petals are yellow and spiralled. It is found in humus at the base of trees at Namgwiri, Bvumbwe.
Flowers February.

Fig. 5. **Liparis neglecta** Schltr. (68)
  About 15 cm tall and found growing at the foot of trees on most of the mountains of Malawi. The two lower leaves are broadly lanceolate and satiny, while the ones on the stem are small and bract-like. The flowers are a greenish-ochre in colour. The sepals are very narrow, the petals broader. The lip is heart-shaped with a dark metalic mid-vein.
Flowers January to March.

Plate 29 Orchidaceae

Plate 30   Orchidaceae

59

Plate 30   Orchidaceae

Satyrium is another large genus of terrestrial orchids, but unlike most orchids, the flower is not twisted through 180° so that the lip is actually at the top of the flower and bears the two spurs which make the satyriums easily recognised.

Fig. 1. **Satyrium buchananii** Schltr. (34)

The pure white flowers of this orchid are very attractive. The lip is hooded, turns back at the tip and has two slender spurs 7 cm long. Sepals and petals curve downwards. The stem is sheathed by bract-like leaves which may be green or pinkish-brown. The foliage leaves are on a sterile shoot. The plant stands 20-35 cm tall and grows in wet grassland and dambos on Nyika and Zomba Plateaux and also on Dzalanyama and Chongoni.
Flowers December to February.

Fig. 2. **Satyrium neglectum** Schltr. (74)

A tall species up to 90 cm with pale or dark pink flowers. The hooded lip has a recurved tip and slender spurs, and the sepals and petals are curled inwards. The bracts are green, pinkish and irridescent. The flower stem is covered with bract-like leaves, while the sterile stem has two to five broad leaves. Found on Zomba Plateau and Nyika growing under pine and in dry grassland.
Flowers February to June.

Fig. 3. **Satyrium atherstonei** Reichb.f. (48)

An attractive orchid. The hood is white with two short spurs close to the ovary. The sepals and side petals are also white, while the centre petal is yellow. The bracts are large and green heavily edged with white, spreading out beyond the flowers and curving down as they mature. The stem is sturdy, sheathed by bract-like leaves, while the foliage leaves are on a sterile stem. Found in wet grassland on Nyika and Zomba Plateaux and round Dedza, Mzimba and Mzuzu. It is usually 30-45 cm tall but I have seen some very fine specimens at Rumphi 90 cm high.
Flowers December to March.

Fig. 4. **Satyrium breve** Rolfe (51 & 429)

An orchid which varies considerably in size in the same locality, not only in height which is from 30-75 cm, but in the size of the flowers. These are in a short dense inflorescence, and may be pale or dark pink with darker markings. The hood has two short stubby spurs. The petals and sepals extend forward and the bracts spread outwards. The stem is ridged. Found in marshy ground on Nyika and Zomba Plateaux.
Flowers October to February.

Fig. 5. **Satyrium anomalum** Schltr. (457)

A very slender orchid up to 1 m tall. Flowers are white, pink or mauve. The hooded lip has two spurs which, unlike most satyriums, fly upwards and outwards like a pair of horns. There are bract-like leaves up the stem and a sterile foliage shoot. Found in grassland and Brachystegia woodland on Zomba Plateau, Soche, Michiru and Dedza Mountains and Nkhota Kota escarpment.
Flowers December to February.

Plate 31   Proteaceae

Although the greatest range of Proteas comes from South Africa, there are several species growing in Malawi. These include a beautiful large scarlet one on the Nyika escarpment, *P. rupestris*, and a miniature one *P. heckmanniana* Engl. on the Nyika Plateau.

Protea angolensis Welw. (608)

The plant illustrated is found near Blantyre but is probably the widest spread of all Protea. It is a handsome shrub up to $2\frac{1}{2}$ m tall. The silky white centre is surrounded by green bracts with rosy pink tips.

Flowers March to September.

Plate 31 Proteaceae

Plate 32   Loranthaceae

Plate 32 *Loranthaceae*

Fig. 1. **Loranthus curviflorus** Benth. (227)
Loranthus is a genus of parasitic plants. This one is found growing on Acacia trees. The leaves are long, narrow and leathery. The flowers have a short tube which opens into six long slender petals which are bright cherry red, filaments and style also red and extended. Often seen round Blantyre.
Flowers intermittently throughout the year.

Fig. 2. **Loranthus blantyrianus** Engl. (162)
Quite commonly seen growing on the same trees as the previous species. The leaves are round to oval and blue-green in colour with a pale bloom. The flowers are greenish-yellow turning orange and russet at the tips. The tube is long and narrow opening into two or three short petals. The style is prominent.
Flowers April and May.

Fig. 3. **Loranthus albizziae** De Wild (228)
A larger and heavier species than the last two. It is found on the Vipya and also on the Kirk Range. The stems are thick and woody, and the leaves are tough, ovate-lanceolate with curious circular markings. The flowers are orange-brown and velvety with a long tube divided into five petals which are red on the inside. The prominent style is purple. They are odd-looking flowers like the hairy hands of a monkey.
Flowers May to July.

Plate 33 Ranunculaceae

Fig. 1. **Delphinium leroyi** Franch. (81)

This is a beautiful plant which is found in the Northern Province in the high grasslands of the Nyika Plateau. The large white flowers are tinged with pink or blue, they have a long slender spur and are very fragrant. The leaves are deeply divided. It grows up to 1,2 m tall.

Flowers February to August.

Fig. 2. **Delphinium dasycaulon** Fresen. (82)

The flowers of this species vary from deep blue to pale mauve, often with a green spot at the base of each sepal. The spur is short and stout. There is no scent. It is found in the Northern Province at lower altitudes than *Delphinium leroyi* and as far south as Dedza and Ncheu.

Flowers February to August.

Fig. 3. **Delphinium** sp.

This lovely sky-blue plant was found not far from the entrance in the Nyika Reserve. It is thought to be a hybrid of the two previous species as it was growing near to both of them. It has a fairly long spur and is faintly scented. It is larger than *D. dasycaulon* but slightly smaller than *D. leroyi*.

Flowers February to May.

Plate 33   Ranunculaceae

Plate 34 Ranunculaceae

Plate 34 Ranunculaceae

Fig. 1. **Knowltonia transvaalensis** Szyszyl. (549)
A most attractive plant which grows in profusion on Luchenya Plateau, Mulanje. The stem branches at the top, each stalk carrying a single many-petalled flower which is white or sometimes flushed with pink on the underside. There are narrow bracts at the base of each branch. The leaves are very deeply lobed. The plant is about 90 cm tall.
Flowers April to October.

Fig. 2. **Clematopsis scabiosifolia** (DC.) Hutch. (84)
An erect plant 90-120 cm high with masses of creamy flowers with pink tinges. They have no petals but the sepals are enlarged and petaloid with numerous yellow stamens clustered in the centre. The leaves vary considerably but are usually composed of five leaflets each divided again into three. The fruit is showy, each seed being attached to a long feathery tail which is caught in the wind. It is found on most grassy hillsides.
Flowers November to May.

Fig. 3. **Clematopsis uhehensis** (Engl.) Hutch. (212)
This species differs from the previous one in having only a single terminal flower on a 45-60 cm stem. The flower is larger than *C. scabiosifolia* and the leaves are ovate and tooth-edged. It is found on the Nyika Plateau.
Flowers November to May.

Fig. 4. **Clematis welwitschii** Hiern ex Kuntze (239)
This dainty little climber is not very common and is found scrambling up grasses and low bushes under Brachystegia from Lilongwe, Kasungu and the Vipya and up to Chitipa, but not recorded from the Southern Province. The leaves are deeply divided and the flowers gracefully placed at the ends of long pink stems. The sepals are pure white inside and pink outside, the stamens are profuse with yellow anthers and green filaments.
Flowers April to July.

Fig. 5. **Ranunculus raeae** Exell (425)
The flowers are bright yellow and vary greatly in size. The stem is branched with small leaves at the dividing point. The main leaves are low down and are very deeply lobed. Although usually found on moist ground it also grows in dry grassland over most of Malawi.
Flowers most of the year.

Plate 35 Malvaceae

Fig. 1. **Azanza garckeana** (F. Hoffm.) Exell. & Hillc. (369)

A woody shrub or small tree. The leaves are large and leathery in texture and on long stalks. The flower grows from the axil of the leaf. It is about 8 cm long, yellow flushed with orange and with a dark centre which is not seen as the flower never opens fully. It is found in mixed woodlands and scrub throughout Malawi.

Flowers December to February.

Fig. 2. **Hibiscus fuscus** Garcke (253)

A tall erect shrub found in scrub and forest edges. The flowers are pure white with wide open petals. The stamens, as in all Malvaceae, are fused into a central column, this species has orange anthers near the top with the style protruding and divided into four. The calyx and stems are covered with bronze hairs. It is fairly common over most of Malawi.

Flowers June to October.

Fig. 3. **Hibiscus rhodanthus** Gurke (680)

This gay little plant, usually only 8-25 cm high, makes splashes of colour in the dry grassland and along the roadsides of the Central and Northern Regions. The leaves are small and tooth-edged and the flowers brilliant scarlet and numerous. It grows from a creeping underground rootstock.

Flowers July to November.

Fig. 4. **Pavonia urens** Cav. (251)

A robust plant which grows up to 2 m and is common at forest margins. The pink flowers have a dark centre, the stamens are purple and the style is single. The whole plant is covered with stiff irritating hairs and the stems are tough and stringy. It is wide-spread in **Malawi**.

Flowers April to October.

Fig. 5. **Pavonia patens** (Andr.) Chiov. (265)

A low shrubby plant. The flowers are orange with a dark mark at the base of each petal. The stamen column is curved with the anthers clustered near the top in a one-sided manner. It was found growing in dry sandy soil at Nkuzi Bay on Lake Malawi.

Flowers January to June.

Fig. 6. **Pavonia columella** Cav. (110)

A most attractive small shrub when it is covered with pale pink flowers, unfortunately it has a heavy pungent smell. The leaves may vary on one plant from ovate to cordate and are tooth-edged. The plant is about 90 cm tall and is found at the higher altitudes in scrub and forest margins.

Flowers April to September.

Plate 35 Malvaceae

Plate 36 Crassulaceae

Plate 36   Crassulaceae

Fig. 1. Kalanchoe lanceolata (Forsk.) Pers. (349)
The broad fleshy leaves of this plant are pale grey-green and are covered with fine, creamy hairs. They are opposite and mainly near the ground with a few pairs up the stem which branches at the top. The flowers are bright yellow and grow in a one-sided manner in each branch. The plant is about 60 cm tall. I have found it in pinewoods near Blantyre and under Brachystegia on the Kirk Range.
Flowers July to October.

Fig. 2. Crassula argyrophylla Diels ex Schönl. & Baker (348)
This very attractive little plant is found growing on rocky mountain slopes often under Brachystegia. The rosettes of obovate, convex leaves are succulent and bronze to red in colour, they elongate into a column 6-10 cm high. These bear single or branched stems with clusters of white star-like flowers. It occurs on Mulanje, Ndirande and Dedza Mountains and on Zomba Plateau.
Flowers June to September.

Fig. 3. Crassula globularioides Britten (347)
The flowers of this species are white with red throats. The stems are red, and the leaves are ovate-lanceolate, succulent and flushed with pink, purple, ochre and green. They form rosettes at the base of the flowering stems which grow from creeping branches. The whole plant becomes a very colourful 'cushion' 6-10 cm high. It is often found with Xerophyta on sunny seepage rocks and on rocky outcrops in the grasslands of Zomba and Mulanje Plateaux.
Flowers June to September.

Fig. 4. Crassula alba Forsk. (97)
This Crassula is not as showy as the last two species. It is found in upland grassland and also on Xerophyta. The flowers are small, creamy, in a flat inflorescence at the top of a red stem. The leaves are bright green and clasp the stem in pairs, the lower ones being longer and forming a rosette. The plant is 15-30 cm tall and is found on Mulanje, Zomba, Dedza and Nyika.
Flowers March to June.

Plate 37   Campanulaceae

Fig. 1. **Cyphia** sp. (541)

This dainty little herb twines its way up grasses and low shrubs in forest or open country. The single pink flowers are on short stalks. The calyx forms a many-pointed frill at the base of the corolla tube. There are five petals, two of which have a dark red splash. The leaves are few, small and oval. Found on Dedza and Mulanje Mountains and on Nyika and Vipya.
Flowers March to July.

Fig. 2. **Lobelia intertexta** Bak. (541)

This small plant has deep blue flowers with a white and yellow throat and a dark spot on the two lower petals. The stems and under sides of the leaves are purple. It grows in wet places and seepage rocks on the Plateaux of Mulanje and Zomba and on Nyika.
Flowers April to September.

Fig. 3. **Lobelia blantyrensis** E. Wimm. (560)

This beautiful plant has large showy flowers of a brilliant blue, with white markings at the centre. The leaves are hairy and purple underneath. It is 30-60 cm tall and is endemic to the higher altitudes of Mulanje and Zomba, where it is found growing on shady banks and under damp rocks and trees.
Flowers most of the year.

Fig. 4. **Wahlenbergia virgata** Engl. (169)

About 60 cm tall. The leaves are small and mainly low on the stem, which divides into many wiry branches each bearing a single delicate mauve flower. It is widespread in the grasslands and forest edges of Malawi.
Flowers intermittently throughout the year.

Fig. 5. **Lightfootia glomerata** Engl. (229)

A much-branched little plant about 30 cm high. The stems are stiff with alternate tooth-edged leaves. The flowers have five narrow, blue, pointed petals. Some flowers appear straight off the stem but most are in a terminal group. It grows in grasslands over most of the country.
Flowers April to August.

Fig. 6. **Monopsis stellarioides** (Presl.) Urb. (437)

A small semi-prostrate plant growing in damp ground. The leaves are lanceolate, tooth-edged and grouped in twos or threes. The flowers appear on pinkish stems from the axil of the leaves, they are orange with purple honey-guides. Found by Chagwa dam on Zomba Plateau.
Flowers January.

Fig. 7. **Lobelia mildbraedii** Engl. (244)

This is one of the giant Lobelias in Malawi. Large leaves form a basal rosette, and from these rises a 2,5 m column densely covered with bract-like leaves and the curious flowers, one of which is illustrated natural size. After the flowers are dead the brown column remains like a post in the marshy ground in which it is found on the Nyika.
Flowers May.

Plate 37   Campanulaceae

Plate 38 Droseraceae Nymphaeaceae Lentibulariaceae Orobanchaceae Scrophulariaceae

Plate 38 Droseraceae

Fig. 1. **Drosera madagascariensis** DC. (402)
This grows on sunny seepage rocks. The leaves are spoon-shaped and covered with glistening red glands which catch small insects on which the plant feeds. They form a tight rosette which opens out as the plant matures. The stem is dark and wiry with several buds opening one at a time into deep pink fragile flowers. Found on Zomba and Mulanje.
Flowers December to May.

Nymphaeaceae

Fig. 2. **Nymphaea caerulea** Savigny (484)
A beautiful water lily standing well above its floating leaves. The petals are blue to purple, the sepals greenish inside and dark blue outside. The size varies from 3-8 cm across. The leaves are bright green and shiny. It is found in most permanent still waters.
Flowers February and March.

Lentibulariaceae

Fig. 3. **Genlisea hispidula** Stapf. (606)
A tiny carnivorous plant growing on wet banks and rocks. The single stem is up to 16 cm tall with a small rosette of leaves at the base. The flowers are purple and dull maroon, and the fruit round and shiny.
Flowers May.

Fig. 4. **Utricularia livida** E. Mey. (346)
A smaller plant with white and purple flowers and a small bladder at the base of the stem. Found on Zomba Plateau and elsewhere on seepage rock and stream edges.
Flowers March to July.

Fig. 5. **Utricularia reflexa** Oliv. (605)
Only 2-3 cm high. It grows from underwater trailing stems which are covered with tiny bladders with which the plant catches its food. Flowers are yellow, borne singly at the tip of the stem.
Flowers May.

Orobanchaceae

Fig. 6. **Orobanche minor** Sutton (337)
A parasite growing in damp forest edges. The stem is dull red, the flowers purple and the bracts ochre. Stem and bracts are hairy. There are no leaves. About 45 cm tall it is found over most of Malawi.
Flowers March to August.

Scrophulariaceae

Fig. 7. **Craterostigma lanceolatum** Skan. (412)
The flowers are white with red lines on the three-lobed lower lip of the corolla. The upper lip of the corolla is hooded. The leaves are in a basal rosette with one or two bract-like ones on the 6-15 cm high stem. It is found on wet rocks on Zomba Plateau and in the Chongoni Forest Reserve.
Flowers December to March.

Plate 39 *Scrophulariaceae*

Fig. 1. **Rhamphicarpa tubulosa** (L.f.) Benth. (370)
A low straggling herb with large attractive flowers which vary in colour from palest pink to deep cherry red. The irregular petals open from a long slender corolla tube. The leaves are narrow, lanceolate and opposite. It is found in marshy ground from Blantyre up to the Northern Provence.
Flowers September to January.

Fig. 2. **Striga gesnerioides** (Willd.) Vatke ex Engl. (574)
Only a few cm high, the stems may be single or branched and are covered with shell-like maroon bracts. The flowers appear near the top and are pink with bent corolla tubes. It is found in damp ground and seepage rock on Mulanje, Nyika, Lilongwe and Dedza.
Flowers February to July.

Fig. 3. **Striga pubiflora** Klotzsch (469)
Also a plant of the dambos, this species has an erect upper corolla lip and a three-lobed lower lip which flares down and outwards. The corolla tube is bent and emerges from a narrow tubular calyx. The leaves are small and few. It is about 45 cm tall and is found along the Lake Chilwa Road.
Flowers January to March.

Fig. 4. **Striga asiatica** (L.) Kuntze (441)
Only 6-15 cm tall this cheerful little plant brightens up the dry grassland. Unfortunately, it is a parasite and can do much damage to crops.
Flowers January to May.

Fig. 5. **Cycnum adonense** E. Mey. ex Benth. (411)
A lovely low compact plant which starts flowering before the rains. It is covered with large delicate white flowers which are tinged with pink. When bruised or dried they turn blue-black giving it the common name of ink flower. It is found on grassy mountain slopes over most of Malawi.
Flowers July to February

Plate 39 Scrophulariaceae

Plate 40   Scrophulariaceae

Plate 40 Scrophulariaceae

Fig. 1. **Alectra sessiflora** (Vahl) Kuntze var. monticola (Engl.) Melch. (533)
This plant has light green leaves which are tooth-edged. The bright yellow flowers grow from the leaf axil, the lower ones opening first but only remaining open for a short time. It is about 30 cm high and is found occasionally in dry grassland over most of Malawi.
Flowers May to July.

Fig. 2. **Gererdiina angolensis** Engl. (98)
A beautiful plant found in dambos at high altitude. It is up to 60 cm tall. The buds are dull pink and the calyx dark red, both very glossy. Each flower has a tubular corolla with five bright pink lobes, with only the style protruding. The whole length of the stem is clasped by lanceolate leaves. It is found on Nyika and also on Vipya.
Flowers most of the year.

Fig. 3. **Buchnera pulchra** Skan ex S. Moore (231)
This is a showy little plant which may have a single or a branched stem. The flowers open in a ring round the terminal inflorescence, and are a glowing purple while the buds in the centre of the ring are maroon or navy. The leaves are green or maroon and are opposite or alternate. It is common in the dry grassland of Nyika and on the Misuku Hills.
Flowers November to July.

Fig. 4. **Buchnera hispida** Buch.-Ham. ex Don (613)
The flowers have purple corolla lobes and greenish tubes. Leaves are small on the upper stem, but the lower ones are much larger and maroon in colour. The plants are 30–40 cm tall. It is found on stony ground under trees along the Michiru road and at Chikala and Mulanje.
Flowers April to June.

Fig. 5. **Buchnera similis** Skan (157)
A slender herb 30–45 cm high with spikes of white or pale mauve tubular flowers with five rather pointed corolla lobes. It turns black when pressed and shrinks considerably in size. It occurs frequently on the plateaux of Mulanje.
Flowers most of the year.

Fig. 6. **Sopubia ramosa** (Hochst.) Hochst. (96)
A dainty little shrub with stiff branches bearing whorls of spiky leaves up their entire length. From these appear two to five delicate pink, irregular flowers, the centres are deep red and the four stamens are joined by the almost black anthers, the stigma is long and curved. The shrub is about 1 m high and is common on grassy slopes and Brachystegia woodlands.
Flowers March to June.

Plate 41   *Solanaceae*

Fig. 1. **Solanum panduriforme** Drège ex Dun.   (197)
A common plant of grassland and roadside. The leaves are ovate, alternate or opposite. The corolla is pale mauve with five lobes. The yellow stamens form a close column. There are a few hook-like prickles on the stem and the fruit is a shiny yellow berry. The height is very variable, from 30 cm to 1,5 m. It is found all over Malawi.
Flowers most of the year.

Fig. 2. **Datura innoxia** Mill.   (315)
A softly hairy, shrubby plant about 1 m tall, with large oval leaves which are asymmetrical at the base. The white trumpet-shaped flowers are 18 cm long and 8 cm across, and have curious 'hooks' between the petals. The fruit is round and spiky with a saucer-shaped surround. It was found growing in sandy soil by the river at Lisungwe Bridge, west of Matope.
Flowers July and August.

Fig. 3. **Nicandra physalodes** (L.) Gaertn.   (482)
Like so many of this family there is an extraordinary variation in size of this plant. I have found seemingly full grown plants in flower of only a few cm, and other plants 3 m tall with stems like small trees. The flowers are lavender-blue with greenish throats and a dark blue spot at the base of each corolla lobe. The fruit is a berry concealed in an inflated calyx. It is widespread throughout Malawi, and, in fact, has become a weed in most parts of the world although it originally came from South America.
Flowers most of the year.

Fig. 4. **Physalis peruviana** L.   (188)
This varies from a few cm to 1,5 m. The leaves are large, alternate and grey-green. The flowers are yellow with maroon markings near the throat. The fruit is a berry in an inflated calyx. It is found round Blantyre, Zomba and Mulanje.
Flowers February to April.

Plate 41   Solanaceae

Plate 42 Acanthaceae

Plate 42   *Acanthaceae*

Fig. 1. **Asystasia gangetica** (L.) T. Anders. (129)
Found scrambling through bushes on the edge of forests and in grasslands. The flowers are white or very pale purple with markings on the lower corolla lip. They grow in a one-sided manner up a short raceme. The leaves are ovate. It is common throughout the country.
Flowers intermittently most of the year.

Fig. 2. **Blepharis grandis** C.B.Cl. (19)
A procumbent herb with long trailing stems on which are borne clusters of blue flowers, each with a single three-lobed corolla lip set amongst sharp prickly bracts. It is a showy plant found in dry scrub and grassland from Dedza northwards.
Flowers April to June.

Fig. 3. **Dicliptera leonotis** Dalz. ex C.B.Cl. (130)
A very attractive though rather straggling plant found on mountain slopes and in light woodland. Each inflorescence is 8-10 cm long having flowers with a purple two-lipped corolla. The stamens are prominent and are joined to the lower lip of the corolla. The calyx is stiff, pointed, pale green and outlined in maroon. The plant may reach a height of 1 m. Found on the Kirk Range.
Flowers April to June.

Fig. 4. **Isoglossa grandiflora** C.B.Cl. (259)
An untidy plant 90 cm to 1,5 m tall. The corolla is divided into two purple lips, the upper lip curving forward forming a hood while the lower one curves downwards and is deeply ridged. The leaves are ovate and turn an attractive scarlet while the plant is still in flower. It is found along mountain streams and is widespread though not very common.
Flowers June to August.

Fig. 5. **Ruellia prostrata sensu** T. Anders. (408)
The pale purple flowers with their long corolla tubes, and five long lobes, grow either terminally or from the axil of the lanceolate leaves. It is an attractive little plant about 30 cm tall found in the Brachystegia hillsides of Michiru, Zomba and as far north as Vipya and Nyika.
Flowers November and December.

Fig. 6. **Justicia striata** (Klotzsch) Bullock (137)
Grows where there is support from surrounding shrubs and grasses. Flowers vary considerably from white to pale mauve or magenta. The corolla has one tiny hooded upper lip and a large three-lobed lower one. The leaves also vary from narrow to broadly lanceolate, often on the same plant. It is widespread.
Flowers most of the year.

Plate 43   Acanthaceae

Fig. 1. **Barlaria senensis** Klotzsch (258)

Growing in very dry grassland and also on the Lake Shore, this is a cheerful plant with heads of prickly green bracts which are grey on the under side. From these appear bright orange tubular flowers with irregular corolla lobes. The stamens and stigma are long and curved, and the leaves are lanceolate. Found at Nkudzi Bay.
Flowers May and June.

Fig. 2. **Dyschoriste hildebrantii** (S. Moore) S. Moore (79)

A lovely small shrublet found on the Mwanza escarpment on the Kirk Range where it flowers profusely, and also on Brachystegia hillsides as far north as Nyika. The woody stems have short branches bearing several pairs of leaves. Flowers spring from the leaf axil, three or four appearing together. The slender corolla tube and lobes are lavender-coloured with purple honey guides, and the calyx maroon and spiny.
Flowers February to September.

Fig. 3. **Barlaria spinulosa** Klotzsch (150)

A rather untidy, many-branched bush up to 1,8 m tall. Flowers have long corolla tubes with irregular purple lobes. The calyx are spiny, pale green with heavy maroon veining, and there are sharp bracts on the reduced shoots in the axil of the leaves; these may easily be mistaken for thorns. It is found along streams and in Brachystegia woodland over the greater part of Malawi.
Flowers April to September.

Fig. 4. **Thunbergia lancifolia** T. Anders. (276)

A small erect plant about 45 cm tall. The leaves are lanceolate light green and shiny. The corolla is a deep purple with a maize-coloured throat and inflated tube. The calyx is covered with minute glistening hairs. It is very showy and is found on many grassy hillsides from Blantyre to as far north as Mzimba.
Flowers June to January.

Fig. 5. **Thunbergia kirkiana** T. Anders. (285)

This low semi-procumbent plant has surprisingly large flowers. The corolla is pure white with a narrow yellow tube. The leaves are arrow-shaped. It is found hanging over banks and in the grasslands of Michiru, Nirande and Zomba.
Flowers January and February.

Fig. 6. **Crossandra greenstockii** S. Moore (752)

The opposite leaves have two pairs of smaller leaves growing from each axil. The terminal heads have squared off prickly bracts out of which grow the flowers with brilliant orange corolla with a single five-lobed lip. The plant is up to 30 cm tall and is found at Likabula, Mulanje and along the Zomba road and occasionally as far as Ncheu.
Flowers November to January.

Plate 43 Acanthaceae

Plate 44 Capparaceae Polygonaceae Amaranthaceae

87

Plate 44 Capparaceae

Fig. 1. Cleome hirta (Klotzsch) Oliv. (261)

A shrubby plant with tiny palmate leaves. The flowers have four pinkish-purple 'stalked' petals, the two outer ones having a central red line, the inner ones having yellow centres outlined in navy. The ten very long graceful stamens curve up from below the petals. It is found from Zomba through to Nyika and along the Lake shore.
Flowers March to September.

Fig. 2. Cadaba kirkii Oliv. (266)

A low shrub with greyish-green, elliptic leaves and sticky green flowers in a terminal inflorescence. There are four petals, long stamens and a curved stigma which elongates into a velvety pod. Usually found on low, sandy flats and amongst termite mounds from Chikwawa through to the Lake and on the Kirk Range.
Flowers May to October.

Polygonaceae

Fig. 3. Polygonum strigosum R. Br. (203)

The spikes of tiny pink and white shell-like flowers are a feature of every dam and stream where this plant grows with its roots in water. The leaves are narrowly lanceolate and alternate, their base enclosed in a sheath which is hairy, brown and striped.
Flowers most of the year.

Amaranthaceae

Fig. 4. Achyranthes aspera L. (308)

A straggling branched weed of scrub and disturbed land. The leaves are opposite or alternate. The flowers are small, dark red and in narrow spikes. The bracts are pinkish-green to straw coloured.
Flowers May to October.

Fig. 5. Amaranthus hybridus L. subsp. **incurvatus** (561)
    (Tim. ex G. & G.) Brenan var. **cruentus** (L.) Mansf.

Another weed of cultivated land. The tall branched inflorescence carries hundreds of minute dark red flowers. The leaves are broadly lanceolate and stalked.
Flowers May to August.

Fig. 6. Aerva leucura Moq. (544)

Found in grassland and roadsides. It grows to 60 cm high, the stems are stiff, the leaves hairy and alternate. The flowers are in dense axillary spikes and are white and woolly.
Flowers March to September.

Plate 45   Asclepiadaceae

Fig. 1. **Stathmostelma pauciflorum** (Klotzsch) K. Schum.   (474)

A dainty little herb with a few flowers at the top of a slender reddish stem. Petals are bright orange and curve upwards. Sepals are a dull red and curve down. The leaves are linear and mainly near the base of the plant. It is about 40 cm tall and found in damp ground round Zomba, Dedza and Nyika.

Flowers September to February.

Fig. 2. **Stathmostelma spectabile** (N. E. Br.) Schltr.   (421)

This is a very striking species, standing about 80 cm high. The umbels of cardinal-red flowers are 18 cm across. The corona is green with yellow and green lobes. The petals are narrow and turn up but are recurved at the tip. The stems become angular when they mature, and the leaves are opposite, ovate and pointed. It is not very common but may be found round Limbe, Magomero, Zomba and on the Lilongwe-Selima road.

Flowers January and February.

Fig. 3. **Ceropegia papillata** N. E. Br.   (101)

An extraordinary-looking little climber. The hanging clusters of flowers have a light brown calyx with darker spots enclosing the green swollen base of the slim corolla tube, this opens into a curious 'cage' formed by the black and green corolla lobes. It is found twining up shrubs at the edge of forests on Zomba Plateau and on Mulanje.

Flowers February and March.

Fig. 4 **Trachycalymma cristatum** (Decne.) Bullock   (688)

Usually only 8-30 cm tall, this herb is found in montane grassland. Petals are green or mauvish green, the corona is white with purple lobes. It is found from Mulanje through Blantyre and Zomba and on to Nyika.

Flowers October to January.

Fig. 5. **Ceropegia filipendula** K. Schum.   (382)

The short, erect flower stems rise straight from the ground bearing two or three pairs of large, narrowly ovate leaves. At the top of each stem is a single pale green flower 10 cm long. It has a slender corolla tube which is swollen at the base and opens at the top into a 'cage' formed by the corolla lobes which are edged with maroon and fold outwards. I found only one plant on Michiru Hill and it was about 20 cm high.

Flowers December.

Plate 45 Asclepiadaceae

Plate 46   *Asclepiadaceae*

Plate 46   Asclepiadaceae

Fig. 1. **Margaretta rosea** Oliv. (371)
The pale purple flowers are in umbels with maroon calyx and stalks. The leaves are narrowly lanceolate and opposite as in all asclepieds. It is a dainty little plant up to 45 cm tall and is found in the grasslands over most of Malawi.
Flowers most of the year.

Fig. 2. **Pachycarpus lineolatus** (Decne.) Bullock (367)
The leaves of this plant are leathery with a pink mid-rib and pink edges and the stem is brownish. The flowers are a silvery mauve and velvety on the outside of the petals, while inside they are pale green with purplish markings. The corona is green with purple and white lobes. It grows to about 75 cm tall and is found in wooded grassland from Mulanje, Michiru, Zomba through to Kasungu.
Flowers November to January.

Fig. 3. **Glossostelma carsonii** (N. E. Br.) Bullock (146)
Also about 75 cm tall, this species has very long and narrow linear leaves. The flowers are in an umbel and the petals, which are a dull reddish-brown, form a cup with recurved tips. As they hang down a great deal of their attractiveness is lost. They are found on the Mountains of Mulanje, Zomba, Sanjika and Chongoni.
Flowers October to January.

Fig. 4. **Brachystelma togoense** Schltr. (478)
A plant growing low on the ground with rather large leaves edged with maroon. The umbels of flat, 'Starfish'-like flowers have petals with a yellow and khaki geometric design, the centres are orange. The rootstock is a flattened tuber with roots round the sides. It is found in Brachystegia woodland on Ndirande, Soche and Mulanje.
Flowers December.

Plate 47   *Balsaminaceae*

Fig. 1. **Impatiens gomphophylla** Bak. (528)

These quaint flowers are like small red and orange chameleons hanging on slender stems. The spur is inflated, tapering towards the tip and curled up. The helmet-like petal is bright red, side petals are orange edged with red, and the lip three-lobed. The plant grows up to 1 m and is found along streams in mountain forest in the Central and Northern Provinces.

Flowers October to June.

Fig. 2. **Impatiens schulziana** Launert (383)

This forms a dense undergrowth in damp shady places, growing up to 90 cm tall. The leaves are large and shiny with pink mid-ribs, and the stems are succulent, pink or maroon. The flowers have five bright pink petals and a long narrow spur which curves forward. It is found by mountain streams on Zomba Plateau and also on Nyika.

Flowers October to April.

Fig. 3. **Impatiens richardsiae** Launert (189)

A low-growing plant with succulent stems and shiny green leaves edged with soft reddish teeth. The numerous flowers are borne singly on red stalks; they are white to pale pink with orange throats and glossy greenish sepals, the lower one forming a short stout spur. It is found on dry ground on the Nyika Plateau.

Flowers January and also July.

Fig. 4. **Impatiens hochstetteri** Warb. (529)

A dainty little species found by forest streams on Dedza mountain. It is only about 22 cm tall. The petals are pure white, the upper ones large and the lower ones tiny and pointed, and the spur is long, narrow and tipped with pink.

Flowers March.

Plate 47 *Balsaminaceae*

Plate 48   Rubiaceae

Plate 48 Rubiaceae

Fig. 1. **Galium stenophyllum** Bak. (278)

A small herb 30-40 cm tall. The flowers are in compound umbels and are very tiny with straw-coloured petals. Leaves are small, narrow and lanceolate and in whorls of six. It is found growing along roadsides and in grassland over most of Malawi.

Flowers most of the year.

Fig. 2. **Agathisanthemum globosum** (Hochst. ex A. Rich.) (334)
Klotzsch ex Hiern

An erect shrublet with spherical heads of tubular flowers. The corollas are navy blue with five pale blue lobes. The stigma is two lobed and prominent, the calyx bright green. The leaves are opposite, lanceolate and pointed, and the stem very dark. It stands 40-60 cm high. It is found occasionally in the higher Brachystegia woodlands and grasslands from Zomba to Nyika.

Flowers October to June.

Fig. 3. **Gardinia subacaulis** Stapf and Hutch. (682)

This is an exciting plant to find with its large, waxy-white flowers which turn creamy yellow as they mature. The corolla tube is long and slender, and the stigma is thick and protrudes just beyond the six corolla lobes. It is very fragrant. The flower, with a few basal leaves, grows straight out of the sun-baked ground. It is up to 18 cm long and 10 cm across. It is found in woodlands in the Central and Northern Regions. The one illustrated was flowering with *Trichodesma hockii* near Lake Kazune.

Flowers August to December.

Fig. 4. **Kohautia cuspidata** (K. Schum.) Brem. (170)

A showy little herb growing in grass and on exposed rocks on Zomba Plateau. The four-lobed corolla may be blue, violet, pink or magenta. The flowers are borne in clusters at the top of the 20-40 cm stems. Leaves are linear and in pairs as in all Rubiaceae.

Flowers January to May.

Plate 49 Rubiaceae

Fig. 1. **Otomeria elatior** (A. Rich. ex DC.) Verdc. (80)

An attractive plant found growing in marshy ground. The long corolla tube opens into five lobes which vary in colour from deep salmon pink fading to pale pink when mature. The stems are hairy and reach a height of about 1 m. It occurs along streams and dams from Mulanje, Zomba right through to Vipya and Nyika.
Flowers all the year.

Fig. 2. **Pentas geophila** Verdc. (85)

A white star-like flower which appears to grow straight out of the ground. The calyx is in a rosette of basal leaves. The corolla tube is 15 cm long and broadens near the flower, opening into five white lobes with the centre of the tube green. The style is long with a yellow stigma. It is found in open grassland on the Nyika Plateau.
Flowers October to January.

Fig. 3. **Borreria dibrachiata** (Oliv.) K. Schum. (117)

The winged 'forget-me-not' of Rhodesia. It is a much-branched herb, 30-60 cm high. There is a pair of large pointed bracts on either side of each inflorescence. The tubular flowers are usually pale blue or purple but I have found the odd white one near Dedza and a pink one on the Kirk Range. It grows over most of Malawi in grassland and on wooded hillsides.
Flowers October to June.

Fig. 4. **Kohautia coccinea** Royle (527)

This is a dainty species up to 45 cm tall found growing in grassland round Ndirande, Dedza and north to Vipya and Nyika. The leaves are linear, the corolla is four-lobed and may be cerise, pink or red.
Flowers March to July.

Fig. 5. **Pentanisia schweinfurthii** Hiern (299)

This is a small compact, very showy plant, only a few cm high, forming cushions of colour before and after the first rains, particularly on burnt grassland. The heads of flowers are a brilliant blue with slighter darker buds. The leaves are shiny green. The plant grows from a thick trunk-like rootstock which goes deep into the ground. It is found on the roadsides and grassland on Zomba Plateau, Dedza Mountain and on much of the high ground north to Nyika.
Flowers September to May.

Fig. 6. **Pentus longiflora Oliv.** (120)

A plant up to 90 cm tall with many branches. The stems are dark red with terminal umbels of flowers. The long corolla tube is bluish-green, the lobes are white, the buds pinkish-yellow and the stigma is prominent. The leaves are lanceolate. A handsome plant found in forest clearings and grasslands on Mulanje, Chiradzulu and Zomba Plateau.
Flowers December to August.

Plate 49 Rubiaceae

Plate 50   Gentianaceae

Plate 50 Gentianaceae

Fig. 1. **Chironia krebsii** Griseb. (410)

A very showy plant up to 45 cm tall, found growing in dambos. The single stem bears a number of flowers with a brilliant pink five-lobed corolla and yellow stamens and a long stigma. Leaves are spoon-shaped and grow at the base of the plant. It is locally common on Zomba Plateau.

Flowers November and December.

Fig. 2. **Chironia laxiflora** Bak. (00)

I only found one plant on a shady bank near Mwanza on the Kirk Range. It was scrambling through undergrowth and reached a height of about 75 cm. The stems are slender and square, and the leaves heart-shaped and opposite. The flower stalks nearly all branch into three with two tiny bracts on the outside branches. The flowers are bright pink, star-shaped, the style is yellow with a purple stigma, and the stamens yellow with a curious twist.

Flowers July.

Fig. 3. **Swertia johnsonii** N. N. Br. (6)

A very lovely plant which is found commonly on the Nyika Plateau. The stems are about 45 cm tall, maroon coloured, wiry and branched, bearing numerous bell-shaped flowers of pale purple. Each of the five corolla lobes has a glistening 'topaz' nectary at the base. The leaves are mainly basal, narrowly lanceolate, maroon or green, with a few pairs of bract-like leaves at the base of the flower stalks.

Flowers May to September.

Fig. 4. **Sebaea grandis** (E. Mey.) Steud. (485)

For a small plant of 5-15 cm this has comparatively large flowers. They are butter-yellow to apricot with green centres. The calyx is winged. Leaves are ovate-lanceolate and sheathe the stem. It is found on damp paths and grassy edges during the rains over many parts of the country.

Flowers February to May.

Fig. 5. **Sebaea longicaulis** Schinz (10)

This is another marsh-loving plant. It may be 5-30 cm tall. Stem is single or branched with pairs of small heart-shaped leaves clasping its length. The bright yellow star-like flowers only open in full sunshine; they have a winged calyx. It is found by the dams and streams on Nyika Plateau.

Flowers July to October.

Plate 51 Euphorbiaceae

Fig. 1. Euphorbia depauperata Hochst. (309)

A small herb 5-30 cm high. The leaves are alternate, lanceolate, bluish-green, and the stems are pink, several rising from a woody rootstock. The 'flowers' are subtended by two round, flat bracts which are beautifully shaded with orange, yellow, green and purple. The stigma appears from between these bracts. Several of these 'flowers' may spring from one point. They are found on dry stony ground on Dedza Mountain, and on Mulanje, Zomba and Nyika Plateaux.
Flowers June to November.

Fig. 2. Euphorbia hirta L. (548)

A very common weed either prostrate or erect. The stems are green or red and the leaves green with a dark brown splash in the centre. The flowers are minute, greenish-brown, forming dense, rounded heads at the leaf axils. It grows from 15-30 cm tall and is found all over Malawi in grasslands and cultivated ground.
Flowers most of the year.

Fig. 3. Euphorbis zambesiana Benth. (325)

A charming little plant only 5 cm high. There are numerous bright red stalks growing from a woody rootstock. Each stalk bears one or two inflorescences with five pinkish-white glands round the edge, and one or two dull green opposite or alternate leaves. It is found on hard dry ground after firing in many parts of Malawi.
Flowers July to November.

Fig. 4. Acalypha stuhlmannii Pax (767)

A common weed of the roadsides, disturbed ground and open grasslands. The male and female flower are found on different plants which are about 30 cm tall. Fig. 4 (*a*) The male flowers are like reddish catkins on stalks growing from the leaf axil. Fig. 4 (*b*) The female flower is composed of a deep red 'mop' of hairy stigmas. It is found widespread throughout Malawi.
Flowers most of the year.

Cactaceae

Fig. 5. Rhipsalis baccifera (J. Miller) Stearn (00)

This succulent herb is epiphytic on trees and rocks in the rain forest and seepage areas of Zomba Plateau, Thyolo and Mulanje. The stems are grey-green forming a low semi-erect shrublet covered with flesh-coloured five-petalled flowers. It later grows long and trails over great distances.
Flowers December and January.

Plate 51 Euphorbiaceae Cactaceae

Plate 52   Boraginaceae

Plate 52   Boraginaceae

Fig. 1. **Cynoglossum geometricum** Bak. & C. H. Wright (126)

A much-branched plant up to 1-2 m in height, with broadly lanceolate leaves. The stems branch at the top bearing small bright blue flowers with purple centres. They grow in a one-sided manner on the raceme. The fruit has four one-seeded parts covered with small spiny hooks. Occurs in forest edges and in grasslands on Ndirande, Zomba, Mulanje and Njika.
Flowers April to July.

Fig. 2. **Trichodesma hockii** De Wild. (681)

A really lovely plant found in dry grassland from Zomba, where it is rare, to Lilongwe and Kasungu, where it is common, and on to Nyika. The flowers are an intense sky blue with green centres and shiny golden glands at the bases of the corolla lobes. They do not hang down like *T. physaloides* and are much larger. The plant is more compact and bushy and stands about 45 cm tall.
Flowers August to December.

Fig. 3. **Trichodesma physaloides** (Fenzl) A. DC. (275)

One of the first spring flowers to appear. They grow in clumps of several branched stems, each bearing numerous white bell-shaped flowers with dark reddish-brown calyx. The stems are smooth and red and the leaves shiny and light green. This is a very attractive plant found over most of Malawi.
Flowers July to December.

Fig 4. **Trichodesma zeylanicum** (Burm.f.) R. Br. (88)

The leaves are opposite, broadly lanceolate and pointed, covered with short stiff hairs and with white glands on the upper surface. The flowers are not as showy as the previous two species. They are small pale blue with pink centres and stiff hairy calyx. The plant is 45-60 cm tall and is found over most of Malawi in grassland and light woodland but more particularly as a noxious weed of cultivation.
Flowers February to August.

Plate 53   Labiatae

Fig. 1. **Pycnostachys**. Variant of **P.urticifolia** Hook. (335)
I found only one plant on Ndirande. It had been bulldozed up during road construction. I rescued it and planted it in my garden where it grew from 45 cm to 3 m tall the following year. The flowers are pure white with two stamens and orange anthers. There are four shiny, pale green bracts below the rounded terminal inflorescence. The leaves are also pale green and shiny and the stems are square as in nearly all Labiatae.
Flowers May to August.

Fig. 2. **Pycnostachys urticifolia** Hook. (192)
This has flowers of a most glorious blue with purple buds forming a sharply-pointed conical inflorescence. The leaves are ovate, tooth-edged with a dull green surface while the young leaves are tinged with maroon. It will grow into a bushy plant up to 3 m tall and is common in grassland and forest margins.
Flowers May to August.

Fig. 3. **Pycnostachys stuhlmanni** Gürke (191)
It is a lovely sight to see these growing in mass along a stream. Each plant is covered with sky-blue flowers on slender maroon stalks. The leaves are very narrow near the top of the plant but broader near the base. It stands about 1,5 m tall, and is found in dambos from Mulanje, Kasungu and Mzuzu.
Flowers April to July.

Fig. 4. **Scutellaria paucifolia** Bak. (108)
Attractive when young and compact but becoming rather straggling, with buds up the length of the long stems, only a few opening at a time. The corolla has a deep purple upper lip and a pinkish lower one. A plant of the upper grasslands of Malawi.
Flowers July to December.

Fig. 5. **Acrocephalus callianthus** Briq. (135)
A most attractive plant. The flowers are rather small and insignificant but the bracts enclosing the rounded inflorescence are pale or sometimes deep purple. Immediately below these are several bracts of the same colour with green tips, while the stem leaves are green. The plant is bushy and about 75 cm tall. It is found in damp shady ground along streams and forest edges.
Flowers April to September.

Fig. 6. **Geniosporum paludosum** Bak. (133)
About 1 m tall. The flowers are purplish-white with prominent stamens and deep purple calyx. They grow in a narrow spike with two or three bracts immediately below the inflorescence, these are pale purple edged with green. It is found over most of Malawi in damp shady places.
Flowers April to August.

Plate 53   Labiatae

Plate 54 Labiatae

Plate 54 Labiatae

Fig. 1. Leucas nyassae Gürke (3)

A plant about 15 cm tall. The flowers are in spherical heads towards the end of long, trailing stems. They are pure white and velvety with orange stamens, the leaves are light green, ovate and tooth-edged. The stems are covered with light brown hairs. It is found growing over most of Malawi on steep grassy slopes.

Flowers April to August.

Fig. 2. Leonotis decadonta Gürke (136)

One of the more spectacular of this genus. It grows to a shrub of about 3 m high and 2 m across. The leaves are large, tooth-edged with silvery grey hairs underneath. The stems are square and ridged. The flowers are a brilliant vermillion, soft and velvety, many of them opening at one time from rounded heads of prickly calyces which are placed along the stem. It is found along the higher gullies on Ndirande Mountain, Thyolo Mountain, and Zomba Plateau.

Flowers June to September.

Fig. 3. Aeollanthus njassae Gürke (515)

This is a lovely plant found growing on rocky outcrops in the mountains. Up to 75 cm tall, with stems and bracts deep purple to navy blue and the flowers pale purple with orange anthers extending well beyond the petals. The leaves are round to oval, and are pale green maturing to light brown. The plants on Sombani Plateau, Mulanje, are very fine indeed, the ones on Zomba Plateau are slightly smaller.

Flowers March to September.

Plate 55   Labiatae

Fig. 1. Orthosiphon rubicundus (D. Don) Benth. (269)
A low bushy plant about 30 cm high. The leaves are broadly lanceolate with tooth edges, glossy green but rough to touch. The stalks and calyx are maroon while the flowers with their two-lipped corolla are pale pink and are in whorled racemes. It grows in grassland and light wooded country in Thyolo, Zomba and on Ndirande and Mulanje.
Flowers June and July.

Fig. 2 Becium obovatum (E. Mey. ex Benth.) N. E. Br. (119)
This is found in most parts of Malawi. It grows to 30 cm high, with thin hairy stems and leaves broad or narrow, varying considerably on the same plant. The flowers are pale pink, mauve or white and are arranged in whorls. The corolla is frilly, the stamens long, curved and purple and the calyx maroon. It is found in Brachystegia woodland, grassy slopes and roadsides.
Flowers most of the year.

Fig. 3. Hemizygia bracteosa (Benth.) Briq. (472)
The pure white bracts at the top of the stems are conspicuous above the surrounding grasses. The flowers are in whorls below the bracts, white with long curling stamens and purplish-blue calyx. The leaves are mainly near the base of the plant which is about 60 cm tall. They are found in marshy ground along the Lake Chilwa road and many other parts of Malawi.
Flowers December to July.

Fig. 4. Salvia coccina L. (155)
Although not originally an indigenous plant it has spread over most of Africa and has been accepted as such. The flowers are scarlet with long stamens and are arranged in whorls. The leaves are slightly tooth-edged. It stands 30-45 cm tall and is found in grassland usually near cultivated land.
Flowers February to April.

Fig. 5. Orthosiphon allenii (C. H. Wright) Codd (125)
An attractive plant which is not common. The single stem is 20-30 cm high and is purple with whorls of pale and dark pink flowers. The bracts are dark pink and the calyx purple. The leaves are all basal, broadly lanceolate with a purple mid-rib. These were found in a dambo just north of Dedza.
Flowers December and January.

Plate 55 Labiatae

Plate 56 Geraniaceae Dipsacaceae

Plate 56   *Geraniaceae*

Fig. 1. Pelagonium luridum (Andr.) Sweet (29)

This is an interesting plant in that it has two types of leaves. The first to appear are almost round with shallow lobes and later come the second type which have long stalks and are very deeply lobed indeed. The flowering stem may be 45 cm tall with an umbel of irregular flowers. These are pink or yellowish-brown. The stems and leaves are covered with fine hairs. It is not very common and is found on dry grassy hillsides from Ncheu to Nyika.
Flowers September to November.

Fig. 2. Geranium vagans Bak. (24)

A small compact plant with very divided leaves which turn beautiful shades of red, yellow and orange. The flowers are white with red bracts. It grows abundantly in grasslands and damp places on the Nyika with an eglandular subspecies on Zomba Plateau.
Flowers all the year round.

Fig. 3. Geranium incanum Burm. f. subsp. **nyassense** (Knuth) (623) Laundon

Not unlike the previous species but the plant is more straggling and grows up into low bushes and grasses. The flowers are pink with a few deeper stripes. It is found on Nyika and Vipya.
Flowers March to June.

Dipsacaceae

Fig. 4. Cephalaria pungens Szabo (216)

A robust plant. The stem is covered with fine hairs. The leaves are deeply but irregularly toothed and are mainly near the base of the plant. The terminal inflorescence is densely packed with small white flowers bearing prominent stamens. It is found in montane grassland on Nyika, Vipya, Zomba and the Shire Highlands.
Flowers December to August.

Fig. 5. Scabiosa austro-africana Heine (215)

A graceful herb about 45 cm high. The flower heads are pink or white, the outer flowers having longer petals. Buds and seed-heads have a prickly look owing to the very pointed calyx lobes. The leaves are very deeply cut. It grows on banks, in grassland and light woodland on the Plateaux of Zomba, Nyika and Mulanje.
Flowers May to October.

Plate 57 *Gesneraceae*

Fig. 1. **Streptocarpus buchananii** C. B. Cl. (622)

Unlike most of this genus this is a bushy herb with fleshy stems. The leaves are heavily veined and covered with soft, shiny hairs. The flowers are on long, wiry maroon stalks and are slipper-shaped, the upper petal rolling back and a darker purple than the lower three-lobed one. The fruit is a long narrow pod which splits spirally as in all Streptocarpus. The plant stands about 50 cm tall and is found growing in deep shade on Zomba Plateau below the Mlunguzi Dam wall.

Flowers December to May.

Fig. 2. **Streptocarpus erubescens** Hilliard & Burtt (166)

Found growing on damp rocks in the rain forests of Soche Mountain, Ndirande and Zomba Plateau. The curved stems carry pale pink flowers with deeper pink spots on the long corolla tube. The plant is only 5-7 cm high and has, usually, two broad leaves.

Flowers January and February.

Fig. 3. **Streptocarpus goetzei** Engl. (423)

A magnificent plant, the single leaf sometimes reaching a length of 60 cm is wavy and frilled at the edges. The flowering stems are about 20 cm tall, branching and rebranching, several appearing during the flowering period. The corolla is large, deep blue, tubular opening into five lobes. They grow on wet rocks, banks and the trunks of rain-forest trees on Zomba Plateau, Ndirande, Mulanje and Thyolo.

Flowers December to March but poorer specimens may be found intermittently throughout the year.

Plate 57 Gesneraceae

114

Plate 58 Lythraceae Dioscoreaceae Turneraceae Caesalpiniaceae Tiliaceae

Plate 58 Lythraceae

Fig. 1. **Nesaea floribunda** Sond. (344)

An untidy straggling plant supported by surrounding shrubs and grasses. The flowers are purple with scarlet filaments and orange stamens, they grow in rounded terminal clusters with purplish-green calyx and boat-shaped bracts below them. Bracts, stems and leaves are covered with fine hairs. It is found near the Coronation Dam, Blantyre and also at Zomba, Nyika and Mulanje. Flowers June to September.

Dioscoreaceae

Fig. 2. **Dioscorea quartiniana** Hochst. (409)

A dainty climber with fragrant, dull white flowers grouped in hanging clusters which grow in pairs from the leaf axils. The leaves are trifoliate. Never very common it is, nevertheless, found in Brachystegia woodlands throughout Malawi.
Flowers December to March.

Turneraceae

Fig 3 **Wormskoldia longipedunculata** Mast. (123)

A brilliant little flower which can be found in most parts of the country. It grows in grassland and light woodland, and has a very long flowering period. The petals are orange to vermillion and the pods very long and narrow. The leaves are mostly near the ground with thick maroon hairs at their base and on the lower stem. It is about 35 cm tall.
Flowers September to July.

Caesalpiniaceae

Fig. 4. **Cassia polytricha** Brenan (147)

A bushy little shrublet 30–45 cm high. The alternate leaves have fifty or more pairs of sensitive leaflets. The flowers are bright yellow with pointed red calyx and are borne on individual reddish stems. The pods are narrow, flat and edged with red. It is common over most of Malawi on grassy slopes, roadsides and scrub.
Flowers January to March.

Tiliaceae

Fig. 5. **Sparrmannia ricinocarpa** (Eckl. & Zeyh.) Kuntze (118)

A shrub found on the forest edges of most of the mountains. The flowers which cluster at the tips of the branches are white or very pale pink. The petals turn back over the stem while the numerous stamens are prominently forward. The leaves are vine shaped and the fruit is a prickly burr.
Flowers July and August.

Plate 59   Convolvulaceae

Fig. 1. **Astripomoea malvacea** (Klotzsch) Meeuse (326)

Usually with only one woody stem which branches at the top, these each bear three or four pink or pale purple trumpet-shaped flowers with dark centres. The buds are twisted and the fruit is round with two seeds inside a brown papery pod. The plant is about 60 cm to 1 m tall and is found at the edge of mixed woodlands over most of Malawi.
Flowers July to October.

Fig. 2. **Ipomoea alpina** Rendle (422)

A small compact herb only 10-14 cm tall with narrow lanceolate leaves, these and the stems are covered with fine white hairs. The flowers are apricot in colour and up to 4 cm across. It is an attractive little plant found on rocky windswept outcrops on Zomba Plateau.
Flowers December to February.

Fig. 3. **Hewittia sublobata** (L.f.) O. Kuntze (502)

A prostrate plant which is widespread, hanging over banks and lying across grassy paths. The flowers are large, pale yellow trumpets with dark red throats. The leaves are heart-shaped, and stems pinkish brown.
Flowers most of the year.

Fig. 4. **Ipomoea pes-caprae** (L.) R.Br. subsp. brasiliensis L. van Ooststr. (526)

The strong trailing stems of this species are several metres long. It grows on the sandy shores of Lake Malawi. The flowers are large and showy, pink with dark centres. The leaves are 'cloven' at the tip, fleshy and deeply veined.
Flowers March to October.

Plate 59   Convolvulaceae

Plate 60 Polygalaceae

Plate 60 Polygalaceae

Fig. 1. **Polygala virgata** Thunb. var. decora (Sond.) Harv. (9)

A shrub growing to 1,5 m tall with several branches bearing sprays of bright purple flowers. The standard sepals flare outwards giving a butterfly effect, and the keel has a dark purple tuft at the tip. The leaves are long, narrow and bluish-green. It is found fairly widespread over higher ground in woodland and forest margins.

Flowers April to November.

Fig. 2. **Polygala albida** Schinz (268)

This species may be a little bushy but has usually a single stem about 30 cm tall. The flowers are greenish-white, mainly terminal with a few clusters lower down the stem. The leaves are lanceolate, alternate. It occurs in scrub and grassland widely throughout the country.

Flowers January to July.

Fig. 3. **Polygala macrostigma** Chod. (8)

This is a slender plant about 2 m high with a single or sometimes branched stem. The purple buds open to paler flowers which mature to creamy white and never open very wide. On only very occasional plants did I see any leaves and these were few, long, narrow and mainly near the base of the plant. The one illustrated was one of numbers found in the grasslands and along the roadsides south of Mzimba. It is fairly widespread but more common in the north of Malawi.

Flowers June to November.

Fig. 4. **Polygala sp.** (Possibly a variant of P. macrostigma Chod.) (7)

A lovely shrub 2 m tall. It has many branches with long narrow lanceolate leaves. The many flowerheads grow from the axil of the leaves and are 25-30 cm long bearing numerous large, deep reddish-purple flowers. It is very showy and is seen at its best on the Vipya and the Nyika escarpment.

Flowers May to July.

Fig. 5. **Polygala petitiana** A.Rich. (519)

Often missed as it grows in grassland and is rather grasslike itself. About 60 cm tall, it branches halfway up into a few almost leafless stems, at the top of each is a onesided raceme of small green flowers with brown veining on the upper petal. It is widespread throughout Malawi.

Flowers January to July.

Plate 61 *Papaveraceae*

Fig. 1. Argemone mexicana L. (333)

This has white or pale yellow saucer-shaped flowers, and numerous stamens with yellow anthers surrounding a thick green style with a red stigma. The leaves are bluish grey with white or pink veins, very spiny and exuding a yellow juice when broken. The plant is about 45 cm high and is found in many parts of Malawi especially on disturbed ground.
Flowers most of the year.

Thymelaeaceae

Fig. 2. Gnidia buchananii Gilg (272)

This bushy little herb is up to 40 cm tall, with very small lanceolate, alternate leaves covering the stems. The flower-heads have a hard red involucre which splits down one side from which appear a number of small yellow flowers with pinkish corollas. These are found widespread on higher ground.
Flowers June to December.

Fig. 3. Gnidia chrysantha (Solms-Laub. ex Schweinf.) Gilg (427)

A most attractive plant with its variation of colours which may be yellow, orange, red or mahogany. The flowers are held together by over-lapping bracts of green. Each plant has several stems each with a terminal inflorescence of dozens of small tubular flowers. It is about 30 cm tall and is found in dambos and grassland.
Flowers September to April.

Fig. 4. Gnidia kraussiana Meisn. (23)

A compact plant 15-20 cm tall with several stems growing from a woody rootstock. The leaves are soft green with a 'bloom', and are ovate, alternate and overlapping up the stems. The yellow tubular flowers are in dense terminal heads. These are found on dry ground, especially after burning, on Nyika, Vipya, Dedza and Ntchisi.
Flowers June and July.

Plate 61 Papaveraceae Thymelaeaceae

122

Plate 62   Selaginaceae   Violaceae

Plate 62 Selaginaceae

Fig. 1. **Selago thyrsoidea** Bak. var. nyikensis (Rolfe) Brenan　　　(111)

A lovely small shrub of about 75 cm. The tiny vivid blue flowers grow in dense, branched spikes which cover the plant. The leaves are very narrow and numerous. When in full bloom it attracts instant attention in the dry grassland. It is found, but not common, on the Nyika Plateau.
Flowers May to July.

Fig. 2. **Selago thomsonii** Rolfe var. thomsonii　　　(109)

This plant is about 45 cm tall. The stems have whorls of three to five small aromatic leaves up their length. The top of the stem branches to form a dense, flat flower-head of tiny mauve flowers. It is found on the high ground of the Nyika and Zomba Plateaux and Mulanje Mountain.
Flowers June to August.

Fig. 3. **Hebenstretia dentata** L.　　　(565)

Several slender branches grow from a woody rootstock. They may be 60 cm to 1,2 m tall and are covered with narrow leaves. The terminal inflorescence is a long narrow spike of creamy tubular flowers with a bright orange splash. It is common in eastern Africa from Ethiopia to South Africa and is found on the plateaux and mountain slopes of Malawi.
Flowers April to November.

Violaceae

Fig. 4. **Viola abyssinica** Steud. ex Oliv.　　　(568)

A gay little herb found occasionally, creeping along under damp banks and rocks. There are four petals of the palest purple and the fifth, lower central one, a deep purple. The stubby spur and stems are maroon. It is found in the higher mountains.
Flowers all the year.

Fig. 5. **Hybanthus enneaspermus** (L.) Muell. var. nyassensis (Engl.) N. Robson　　　(357)

A much branched little plant with curious shovel-shaped flowers. There is one large pinky-mauve petal with strongly defined honey guides, and two tiny curled-up petals above. The leaves are narrowly lanceolate and grow irregularly up the stem. The fruit is a capsule. It grows to about 25 cm and is found on Ndirande, Nyambadwe and also in the central region.
Flowers December to February.

Plate 63   Pedaliaceae

Fig. 1. Sesamum angolense Welw. (195)

This is a beautiful plant, often called the 'African Foxglove'. It is 1,5 to 2 m tall with several cane-like stems. These bear large pink flowers either singly or in pairs. The wide corolla tube flares into five lobes, the lower one being the longest and striped with red. The leaves are ovate-lanceolate. It is found very widespread in Malawi where it forms large showy clumps along the roadside.
Flowers March to July.

Fig. 2. Ceratotheca sesamoides Endl. (151)

A small herb up to 25 cm high. The shape of the leaves varies considerably on one plant. The corolla tube is covered with fine hairs, as are the leaves and stems. The seed pod has two horns. It is mostly found in dry ground near Lake Malawi and the Shire River and round Blantyre.
Flowers February to July.

Oxalidaceae

Fig. 3. Oxalis chapmaniae Exell (194)

Not more than 14 cm high, it grows from a small bulbil at the end of an underground stem. The trifoliate leaves have long narrow leaflets. The flowers are in a terminal umbel and are bright pink to magenta with yellow or green centres. It is found in grassland and disturbed ground on the Nyika Plateau where it is endemic.
Flowers May and June.

Fig. 4. Oxalis corniculata L. (610)

This forms a cheerful ground cover on roadsides or in damp and shady forest. The leaves are trifoliate. The flowers are bright yellow and the stems root at the nodes. The plant is only about 10 cm high and is found in many parts of Malawi.
Flowers December to May.

Plate 63   Pedaliaceae   Oxalidaceae

126

Plate 64   Papilionaceae

127

Plate 64   *Papilionaceae*

Fig. 1. **Crotalaria lanceolata** E. Mey. (232)

The inflorescence of this rather straggling herb, is a dense cluster of sulphur-yellow flowers with brown lines on the standard petals. The leaves are trifoliate and narrow and the plant is about 45 cm tall. It occurs on Vipya and the Shire Highlands.

Flowers May.

Fig. 2. **Crotalaria shirensis** (Bak.f.) Milne-Redh. (535)

A tiny bushy little herb 5-10 cm tall. The leaves are long and narrow appearing singly where the stems branch, but are broader and shorter near the base. Stems are wiry, flowers are small and yellow with a few brownish lines on the standard petals. The pods are cylindrical and velvety brown. It is found on Ndirande.

Flowers March.

Fig. 3. **Crotalaria pallida** Ait. (184)

A slender, untidy plant of about 75 cm. The leaves have three leaflets and the usual inflated seed pod of this genus. The flowers are in a long narrow raceme. Each flower has a tall standard petal with tan stripes on the back, wing petals are yellow and the deep keel is brown tipped with green. It is found along the Michiru Road, Blantyre.

Flowers April and May.

Fig. 4. **Crotalaria lachnorphora** A. Rich. (530)

A very showy plant up to 60 cm tall. The leaves are trifoliate on long stalks, silvery grey and covered with fine hairs. The flowers are large, very bright yellow with the standard curving backward, the wing petals are even deeper yellow and the shallow keel is greenish. It is found in the grasslands and along the roadsides round Ncheu.

Flowers March.

Fig. 5. **Crotalaria laburnifolia** L. (607)

The flowers of this species are magnificent. The brilliant yellow standard which curves backwards has tan stripes on the outer side. The wing petals are yellow. The keel is very large, deep and curves to a sharp point, and is the palest of greenish yellow with spotted lines and a brown tip. They hang from thin stalks on a lax raceme. The shrub is from 60 cm to 1,2 m high. It is found round Mwanza on the Kirk Range, Zomba and near Chilaka.

Flowers November to July.

Plate 65 Papilionaceae

Fig. 1. **Macrostyloma axillare** (E.Mey.) Verdc. var.axillare (289)
A small creeper with pale lemony-green flowers. The calyx is brown and pointed and leaves are trifoliate. The pods are long, narrow and bean-like. It is found widespread on higher ground in scrub at forest margins.
Flowers May to January.

Fig. 2. **Sphenostylis stenocarpa** (Hochst. ex A.Rich.) Harms (471)
A gay little creeper which winds its way up grasses and low shrubs. The leaves are trifoliate, the leaflets narrow and pointed. The two to four flowers on each stalk are a bright cerise in colour fading to dull blue and then brown. It is found on high ground over most of Malawi.
Flowers February and March.

Fig. 3. **Dolichos kilimandscharicus** Taub. (167)
This has a brilliant spike of flowers which pushes its way through the dry ground. The colour varies from rich purple, blue to mauve or occasionally, almost pinky white. The leaves which appear later are grey-green with five to seven leaflets. It becomes a small erect herb of about 75 cm. It is found in grassland and under Brachystegia and is widespread throughout Malawi.
Flowers September to January.

Fig. 4. **Amphicarpa africana** (Hook.f.) Harms (165)
A dainty little herb occasionally found growing up shrubs and grasses at forest edges at higher altitudes. The leaves have three oval leaflets and are alternate. The slender flower stalks hang down from their axil, each bearing several small purple, pea-like flowers.
Flowers April to August.

Fig. 5. **Parochetus communis** Buch-Ham. ex D.Don (303)
A charming small herb which forms a ground cover, 15 cm high in damp shady parts of the rain forest. The rounded trifoil leaves have white markings along the centre veins. The flower stems rise well above the leaves and carry one or two pea-like flowers of the most beautiful sky blue. Stems fall back when the pods mature. It is found on Zomba Plateau and Chiradzulu.
Flowers June to September.

Fig. 6. **Vigna pygmaea** R. E. Fries (291)
A tiny species growing out of baked ground, often just a posy of two or three pinkish-purple flowers 2-5 cm high. The leaves, when they appear, are trifoliate, narrow and pointed. They are green or often maroon. It occurs on Ndirande, Zomba Plateau, Dedza and Nyika.
Flowers June to September.

Plate 65 Papilionaceae

Plate 66   Papilionaceae

Plate 66   Papilionaceae

Fig. 1. **Indigofera atriceps** Hook.f. subsp. atriceps (522)
A small branched herb with pinnate leaves usually bearing four pairs of leaflets. The flowers are brick-red to scarlet and grow from dark hairy bracts. The pods are small and cylindrical and are also covered with dark hairs. The plant is about 45 cm high and is found on roadsides and forest edges on Zomba Plateau, Nyika, Vipya and Misuku.
Flowers January to August.

Fig. 2. **Indigofera dendroides** Jacq. (00)
A straggling herb found growing beside roads and in grassland. The inflorescence of salmon-pink flowers is borne on a long slender stalk which rises from the leaf axil. The leaves have five to eight pairs of leaflets. Grows on Zomba Plateau, Nyika and Dedza and Mulanje Mountains.
Flowers March to July.

Fig. 3. **Trifolium simense** Fresen (206)
A herb only 12 cm high found growing on the Nyika Plateau, usually on disturbed ground and along roadsides. The leaves are trifoliate either with or without stalks. The flower-head is spherical and is made up of numerous small pink flowers.
Flowers March to June.

Fig. 4. **Vigna vexillata** (L.) Benth. (223)
Found more or less throughout Malawi. It scrambles amongst grasses and low bushes. The leaves are trifoliate, the leaflets broadly lanceolate and pointed. There are two flowers borne on a long stem, one opening at a time, they are rich purple to creamy brown. The pods are long and straight and covered with fine bronze hairs.
Flowers September to April.

Fig. 5. **Tephrosia nyikensis** Bak. supsp. nyikensis (540)
This is a virgate shrub up to 2 m tall. The purple flowers are in terminal heads. The calyx is covered with silky bronze hairs making the buds appear almost black. The leaves are blue-green with six or seven pairs of leaflets and one at the tip. It is found in forest margins and clearings on Ntchisi, Vipya, Nyika, Mitsuku and as far south as Dedza Mountain.
Flowers March to July.

Plate 67   *Papilionaceae*

Fig. 1. **Mucuna poggei** Taub. var. pesa (De Wild.) Verdc.   (553)

A rampant climber with large trifoliate leaves. The yellowish green flowers are 5 cm long and hang in dense heads like bunches of grapes, 30 cm in length. The calyx and pods are covered with shiny, copper coloured hairs. Beware of these for if you touch them or shake them down onto yourself they will cause intense irritation. It is found in most forests climbing up the highest trees.
Flowers March and April.

Fig. 2. **Mucuna pruriens** (Taub.) DC.   (505)

This is not nearly as vigorous a climber as the previous one. Bunches of seven to ten smaller flowers hang below the leaves. The calyx is pale green, the standard petal dull mauve and the remaining petals a dull purple. They have a putrid smell. The leaves are trifoliate, pods long and slightly curved and like *M. poggei* they are covered with very irritating hairs. It is found scrambling over shrubs and banks around Blantyre, Dedza and Kasungu.
Flowers March and April.

Plate 67 Papilionaceae

Plate 68 Papilionaceae

135

Plate 68   *Papilionaceae*

Fig. 1. **Aeschynomene schimperi** Hochst. ex A.Rich.   (503)

Up to 1,5 m tall, with a rather thick stem covered with soft brown hairs, as are the calyx and pods which are long and narrow. The leaves have twenty or more pairs of leaflets with one at the end. The flowers are striking, a deep orange yellow with a conspicuous keel which is green marked with maroon. It grows in wet shady places. Although not very common it is found widespread in Malawi.

Flowers February to August.

Fig. 2. **Aeschynomene abyssinica** (A.Rich.) Vatke   (93)

This is a very graceful shrub up to 2 m tall with a Japanese look about it. The stems are free of leaves except for the lower branches, they are shiny maroon in colour and very sticky. The flowers are small and numerous with maroon sepals and bright yellow petals, the standard having a few dark stripes. The keel is greenish, and the fruit is in two sections and looks like a small pair of spectacles. A very common plant of Miomba woodland and grassy mountain slopes.

Flowers January to August.

Fig. 3. **Sphenostylis marginata** E.Mey. subsp. erecta (Bak.f.) Verdc.   (292)

A lovely little shrublet, compact and rounded and about 60 cm high. The leaves are trifoliate, light green and stalked. The flowers are dark red, almost black in bud and open to a brilliant yellow with red at the back of the standard. A common and widespread species.

Flowers most of the year.

Fig. 4. **Desmodium repandum** (Vahl) DC.   (148)

An attractive plant of about 60 cm, found in rain forests and shady streams in all three regions. The brilliant flowers have orange-red upper petals, the keel being red above and cream below. The stems are maroon, long and wiry. Leaves grow low down on the plant with three leaflets, rather shiny with fine hairs on top.

Flowers March to July.

Plate 69   Ericaceae

Fig. 1. Blaeria kiwuensis Engl. (235)

A small herb or subshrub about 30 cm high. The leaves are very small, narrow and numerous. The flowers are tiny, pink and bell-like with dark centres. It is found in dry grassland on Nyika and Zomba Plateau and Mulanje Mountain.
Flowers December to June.

Fig. 2. Erica johnstoniana Britt. (576)

A lovely little shrubby herb growing on the peaks of Mulanje Mountain at about 2 500 m. It is up to 36 cm tall. The whole plant is covered with fine silvery hairs. The leaves are small and the flowers are in nodding clusters, forming small pink balls with red centres.
Flowers April to September.

Ochnaceae

Fig. 3. Ochna macrocalyx Oliv. (480)

The flowers of this woody little plant, although a most attractive bright yellow, last such a short time that they are not often seen. The calyx, on the other hand, turns a lovely cherry-red tinged with orange or purple and the large green seeds turn a glossy black and these remain on the plant for a considerable time. The leaves are rather leathery, but shiny. It grows from a woody root-stock and may be from 10-30 cm high. It is found widespread on mountain slopes in all three regions.
Flowers November to March.

Onagraceae

Fig. 4. Ludwigia octovalvis (Jacq.) Raven (467)

A bushy plant about 50 cm tall with long narrow, lanceolate leaves. The stems are reddish brown. The flowers are on short stalks which lead to the long narrow ovary, there are four pointed green sepals and four bright yellow petals. When the flower dies the ovary swells and the seeds disperse leaving a lace-like structure. It is found widespread in dambos and other wet places.
Flowers February to June.

Plate 69   Ericaceae   Ochnaceae   Onagraceae

Plate 70 Verbenaceae

Plate 70 Verbenaceae

Fig. 1. Clerodendrum myricoides (Hochst.) Vatke (196)

An attractive shrub up to 1,2 m tall. The oval leaves are in two's or four's and are slightly hairy. The young leaves are pinkish brown. The corolla has four pale blue lobes with a fifth lobe much darker blue. The four stamens and stigma grow forwards and upwards in a graceful curve. It is found in wooded grassland from Mulanje, Blantyre, Dedza, Mzimba to Karonga.
Flowers October to January.

Fig. 2. Clerodendrum c.f. wildii Moldenke (750)

The flower is not unlike *C.myricoides* in colour but the stamens curve upwards and back. The plant is only 30–45 cm high with a thick woody rootstock, the stems are reddish mauve and velvety and the leaves large and soft. After all the flowers have faded the fruits are most striking, they are round and shiny, green becoming black and are enclosed in a rich purple calyx. It grows on rocky hillsides on Mulanje, Nyambadwe, Rumphi and Nyika.
Flowers September to December.

Fig. 3. Clerodendrum rotundifolium Oliv. (324)

A shrub up to 2 m tall with large felty leaves. The white flowers have slender corolla tubes up to 10 cm long, and stamens which extend 3 cm beyond the five lobes. They are very fragrant and are found at forest edges on Dedza Mountain, Thyolo and Zomba Plateau.
Flowers March to July.

Fig. 4. Lippia javanica (Burm.f.) Spreng. (115)

Growing in light woodland and scrub, this rather subdued shrub has a pungent smell when bruised. Flowers are small, white with yellow centres and grow in an elongated, cone-shaped head. The leaves are rough and tooth-edged. It is about 1,5 m tall and is found over most of Malawi.
Flowers January to May.

Fig. 5. Lantana camara L. (352)

Regarded in many parts of Africa as a noxious weed, this shrub can still be very colourful as the flowers vary from pale yellow and pink to orange and crimson. It is found scrambling to great heights in trees and scrub in light forests and grassland. The fruit is a cluster of shiny black berries. Originally of American origin, it is now widely naturalised in tropical countries and widespread in Malawi.
Flowers all the year round.

Plate 71   Umbelliferae

Fig. 1. **Diplolphium buchananii** (Benth. ex Oliv.) Norman (316)

This very handsome and aromatic plant is a virgate shrub or sometimes almost a small tree. The rounded inflorescence is a compound umbel of greenish-white flowers, each umbel with several pale green bracts. When mature the umbel can be 25 cm across. The base of the leaf forms a sheath enclosing the stem. The typical subspecies is endemic to Malawi and grows on Mulanje Mountain and Zomba Plateau where it is common on rocky cliff edges and grassy slopes.

Flowers May to October.

Fig. 2. **Alepidia longifolia** E.Mey. (193)

A dainty little herb up to 1 m tall although usually much shorter. The leaves are obovate and fringed at the edges, forming a rosette on the ground. The stems branch at the top each bearing a terminal umbel of white bracts with green backs and sessile brownish flowers in the centre. They are found in wet ground on Nyika Plateau and most of the higher areas of the country.

Flowers July.

Fig. 3. **Pimpinella huillensis** Welw. ex. Engl. (513)

A delicate plant of about 90 cm. The compound umbels are formed by tiny white flowers which are pale green before unfurling. The sheaths enclosing the stem are maroon and have three lobes. It grows in grassland and light woodlands on Ndirande, Zomba Plateau and Dedza Mountain.

Flowers March.

Plate 71   Umbelliferae

Plate 72   Melastomataceae

143

Plate 72 Melastomataceae

Fig. 1. **Dissotis melleri** Hook.f. (722)
A spectacular species flowering when little else is out. The large and brilliant flowers are clustered at the ends of the brown leafless stems. The petals are magenta to purple, the filaments red with navy anthers. It grows to about 1,2 m tall. It is endemic to Zomba Plateau and Mulanje where it is found on rocky outcrops, grassland and under Brachystegia.
Flowers May to September.

Fig. 2. **Dissotis debilis** (Sond.) Triana (200)
A slender plant with a terminal inflorescence bearing several small magenta flowers. There are four narrow bract-like leaves immediately below the inflorescence and clusters of leaves up the narrow stem. It is found occasionally in dambos in all three regions.
Flowers most of the year.

Fig. 3. **Dissotis canescens** (E.Mey. ex Graham) Hook.f. (00)
An attractive plant about 1,2 m tall. The flowers are pink to magenta, the stamens have red filaments and purple anthers, the stigma is pale pink. The five lobes of the calyx are brown outside and red inside and are covered with tiny glands. It is found overhanging mountain pools at Likabula on Mulanje, at Thyolo and on most higher ground throughout Malawi.
Flowers July to December.

Fig. 4. **Dissotis senegambiensis** (Guill. & Perr.) Triana (319)
This is a lovely little shrub only 60-90 cm tall. The hairy buds open to light purple flowers, each with ten bright yellow stamens, five upper and five lower ones. The style is pink and the stem square and covered with fine hairs. Found in rain forests and along streams on Mulanje, Zomba Plateau and at Nkhata Bay.
Flowers April to May.

Fig. 5. **Antherotoma naudinii** Hook.f. (149)
Very variable in height, it may be 5 cm with a single stem or 20 cm and branched. The calyx is dark and covered with reddish-orange star-shaped hairs. Common along wet paths and shallow seepage soil amongst rocks and on most of the hills and mountains.
Flowers March to September.

Plate 73 Guttiferae

Fig. 1. Hypericum revolutum Vahl (293)

A tall shrub up to 4 m. The leaves are narrow lanceolate and grow profusely up each woody stem. The large delicate flowers have five bright yellow silky petals, a superior ovary and red style surrounded by numerous stamens. This is a showy bush which gives off a distinct curry smell although this cannot be detected when the flowers or leaves are picked. It is found on high ground at forest edges on Zomba Plateau, Nyika and Mulanje and Dedza Mountains.
Flowers May to January.

Fig. 2. Hypericum peplidifolium A.Rich. (403)

This is a tiny species, 5-15 cm high. It may be bushy or semi-prostrate. The small yellow flowers have orange stamens. It is found in open grassland and roadsides on most of the high ground in Malawi.
Flowers October to February.

Rosaceae

Fig. 3. Rubus ellipticus Sm. (678)

A bramble growing in forest clearings and along grassy paths. The new shoots are very tall, strong and arching, they are covered with stiff red hairs. The flowers are small, pale pink with dark stamens. The fruit is a cluster of orange berries which are sweet and pleasant to taste. A species surprisingly not native but introduced from Asia and well naturalised on Mulanje, Zomba Plateau and Nyika.
Flowers nearly all the year.

Oleaceae

Fig. 4. Jasminum meyeri-johannis Engl. (679)

A shrub with delicate white fragrant flowers, the back of the petals are dull pink and show in the furled bud. It is found hanging over rocks and in mountain gorges on Mulanje Mountain and Zomba Plateau.
Flowers October to December.

Plate 73   Guttiferae   Rosaceae   Oleaceae

Plate 74 Cucurbitaceae

147

Plate 74 Cucurbitaceae

Fig. 1. **Lagenaria sphaerica** (Sond.) Naud.   (267)

A lovely large white flower with petals like crepe-paper, green at the centre. The stamens are clustered on three short stalks and are bright yellow. The leaves are hand-shaped and variously lobed. This is a climber which uses tendrils which are branched. It is found scrambling over banks and bushes on the lower slopes of Ndirande, at Nkudzi Bay, Karonga and Nyika.

Flowers March to July.

Fig. 2. **Momordica foetida** Schumach.   (516)

A dainty little plant which climbs by tendrils up grasses and low shrubs. The leaves are on short stalks, heart-shaped and slightly lobed, and the flowers are on longer stems. A pale wide receptacle tube opens into bright orange petals. The calyx is purplish-black. It is fairly common around Blantyre, Thyolo, Zomba and Dedza.

Flowers January to August.

Fig. 3. **Coccinia adoensis** (Hochst. ex A.Rich.) Cogn.   (487)

Usually found under trees, growing up shrubs and grasses. The corolla lobes are apricot in colour and crinkly in texture. The leaves vary from heart-shaped to hand-shaped. The tendrils are tightly curled. Found at Thyolo, Zomba Plateau, Vipya and Nyika.

Flowers August to February.

Fig. 4. **Trochomeria macrocarpa** (Sond.) Hook.f.   (00)

A delightful little climber, growing from a surprisingly large woody rootstock. The strange flowers have a long green receptacle tube with trailing, yellowish-green petals. There were only one or two tiny leaves on the one plant I found which was on dry baked ground near Nasawa. It has also been found at Dedza and Nyika.

Flowers October to December.

Plate 75   Caryophyllaceae

Fig. 1. **Polycarpaea eriantha** Hochst. ex A.Rich. (511)

A delightful miniature shrublet of the Dianthus family. It is only 5-15 cm tall and is very branched with tiny greenish-grey leaves arranged in whorls up the stems, and two or three broad leaves at the base of the plant. The flowers are in terminal clusters, they are very small and silvery-pink. It is found in dry grassland and along roadsides round Blantyre and Zomba.
Flowers March.

Compositae

Fig. 2. **Helichrysum setosum** Harv. (290)

This is a very showy plant up to 90 cm. The leaves are both alternate and opposite, brownish-green and rough in texture. The flowers are yellow maturing to brown and are enclosed in brilliant golden bracts. It occurs quite widely in the higher grasslands, including Zomba Plateau, Matandini on the Kirk Range where there are some very fine specimens, Dedza, Vipya and Nyika.
Flowers May to August.

Fig. 3. **Helichrysum herbaceum** (Andr.) Sw. (15)

A small species about 25 cm high. The stems occasionally branch to bear several terminal flower-heads, but usually bear just one single head. The bracts open very wide and are a bright silvery gold inside and golden brown outside, glistening when they catch the sun. The leaves are grey-green, very narrow and grow numerously up the stem. Found in open grassland on Nyika and Vipya Plateaux.
Flowers March to July.

Fig. 4. **Helichrysum lastii** Engl. (107)

A straggling herb with small alternate leaves which curl at the tip, they and the stems are blue-grey and are covered with fine silvery hairs. The terminal inflorescence is made up of many tightly packed, small yellow flowers. The plant forms an attractive ground cover in the grasslands and rocky outcrops of Zomba Plateau, Ndirande and Mulanje Mountain.
Flowers May and June.

Fig. 5. **Helichrysum patulifolium** Bak. (13)

A showy little shrub up to 45 cm. It is covered with numbers of small round flower-heads whose bracts are yellow or orange with tips which turn outwards. The leaves are small narrow, and grey-green, and cover the stems. It is found in the grasslands of Nyika and Vipya Plateaux.
Flowers June to October.

Plate 75   Caryophyllaceae   Compositae

Plate 76　Compositae

Plate 76 Compositae

Fig. 1. Helichrysum whyteanum Britten (112)

One of the loveliest of the Helichrysums. It is a bushy plant 60-90 cm tall, growing at high altitude on rocky outcrops on Mulanje Mountain where it is endemic. The bracts are a glistening white often with a very delicate pink tinge, while the flowers are pale brownish-yellow. The leaves are small and closely spaced up the stem, which, like the backs of the leaves are covered with soft silvery hairs.

Flowers May to November.

Fig. 2. Helichrysum flammeiceps Brenan (12)

Forms dense bushes 30-40 cm high on the sloping grasslands of the Nyika Plateau, they are especially fine near Kasaramba where the ground is aglow with these delightful plants. Each little bush is so covered with flower-heads which vary from yellow to orange, mahogany and purple-red, all with yellow tips, that they seem to be on fire. The leaves are very narrow, dull green and numerous.

Flowers June to August.

Fig. 3. Helichrysum brassii Brenan (587)

Found under shelter of rocks and in shallow soil on rocky outcrops on the peaks and in the plateau grasslands of Mulanje Mountain. The leaves are broadly lanceolate, brownish-green above, silver below. The flower-heads are bright yellow with the outer bracts tipped with black. This is another very attractive species with its contrast in colour.

Flowers April to September.

Fig. 4. Helichrysum nitens Oliv. & Hiern (139)

The large silvery leaves which may be 22 cm long, form rosettes on the ground. From these appear a single stem, 60-100 cm tall, at the top of which are six to a dozen or more large flower-heads with gleaming golden bracts. This is a very handsome species which is far more showy at the higher altitudes. It grows on Zomba Plateau and the Nyika but is much finer on the plateaux of Mulanje. The leaves illustrated are one-third natural size.

Flowers March to October.

Plate 77 Compositae

Fig. 1. **Veronia adoensis** Sch.-Bip. ex Walp. (142)
A woody shrub up to 1,5 m tall. The leaves are alternate, lanceolate, rough and greyish on the underside. The inflorescence has cream and green bracts with pale mauve tubular flowers with prominent stamens. Found on most of the mountains in grassland bordering forests.
Flowers February to September.

Fig. 2. **Vernonia superba** O.Hoffm. (254)
This is an attractive plant growing to about 1,2 m tall. It is much branched but has few leaves and these mainly at the base of the plant. The inflorescence is made up of numerous tubular flowers of a startling sky-blue, they are enclosed in pale green bracts which are recurved. Found in grassland and forest edges round Blantyre and Dedza.
Flowers March and April.

Fig. 3. **Vernonia chloropappa** Bak. (208)
A charming little herb, 30 cm tall. Flower-heads are borne singly on a slightly branched stem. The flowers are all tubular, white or pink, while the pappus on the fruit is bright emerald green. Leaves are alternate and few. Found under Brachystegia in the north of the country.
Flowers May to September.

Fig. 4. **Vernonia poskeana** Vatke & Hildebr. (164)
This dainty little species grows up to 60 cm. The flowers are a deep reddish purple, a great number of heads opening at a time. There are several branching stems with narrow lanceolate leaves making a compact, small and colourful shrublet. It is found in most grasslands.
Flowers May to September.

Fig. 5. **Vernonia gerberiformis** Oliv. & Hiern (100)
The single, terminal flower-head is borne on an unbranched stem only 2-10 cm high, covered with fine hairs and bearing one leaf-like bract. The involucral bracts are large and overlapping, and the rich purple tubular flowers form a 'mop' with their extended stigmas. The leaves are on long pinkish stalks all growing from the base of the plant which is very like a Gerbers. Found in grassland and disturbed ground along roadsides on Dedza Mountain and on Nyika.
Flowers July to January.

Fig. 6. **Vernonia petersii** Oliv. & Hiern (179)
The stems have irregularly placed lanceolate leaves. The flowers are tubular, deep purple with white anthers, while the involucre is covered with grey woolly hairs. It stands 30-60 cm high in grassland in most parts of the country.
Flowers April to August.

Plate 77   Compositae

154

Plate 78   Compositae

155

Plate 78 Compositae

Fig. 1. **Berkheya zeyheri** (Sond. & Harv.) Oliv. & Hiern (143)
The bright yellow flower-heads are surrounded by very prickly bracts. The leaves are long, narrow, deeply lobed and are also very spiny, most of them growing near the base of the plant. It is about 45 cm high and is found in the upper grassland and Plateaux of Malawi.
Flowers October to January.

Fig. 2. **Hypericophyllum scabridum** N.E. Br. (207)
A very handsome plant growing up to 90 cm with flower-heads 4 cm across. These consist of only tubular florets which are a glowing orange to vermillion in colour with prominent, lighter coloured two-lobed stigmas. The bracts are purplish-brown. The leaves are dull bluish-green with purple mid-rib and edges. It is found on Ndirande, Mulanje and also in the Northern Region.
Flowers April to August.

Fig. 3. **Bidens steppia** (Steetz) Sherff (91)
A cheerful annual plant with a very long flowering period. The bright yellow ray-florets are deeper in colour towards the base. The leaves are opposite and deeply cut. It is found in most grasslands, roadsides and forest edges. Size of the plant varies in height from 30 cm to 2 m.
Flowers March to October.

Fig. 4. **Inula glomerata** Oliv. & Hiern (296)
A striking plant of unusual colouring, covered with velvety hairs which vary from silver to rusty brown. The stem is strong and branched at the top, the flower-heads clustered at the ends of the branches and in the axil of the leaves. They are orange with brown bracts. The leaves at the base of the plant are very large indeed, they may be 22 cm wide and 60 cm long, and the plant may be 2 m tall. Found widespread throughout Malawi.
Flowers June to September.

Fig. 5. **Anisopappus lastii** (Hoffm.) Wild subsp. lastii (575)
A tiny much branched herb which forms sheets of colour on seepage rocks on Mulanje. The flower-heads are orange, conical and numerous with no rays.
Flowers April.

Fig. 6. **Osteospermum monocephalum** (Oliv. & Hiern) T.Norlindh (620)
A plant 45-80 cm tall with slender stems carrying brilliant yellow flower-heads, and later, very attractive seed-heads. Each seed is green with a shiny pink membrane round it and together they look like small coloured lanterns. It is found in grassland and light woodland over most of Malawi.
Flowers May to October.

Fig. 7. **Emilia javanica** (Burm.f.) Merr. (145)
A gay little herb which is found in grasslands in most parts of Malawi. The stem is about 45 cm tall, branches near the top, each branch carrying a single head of tubular flowers only. These are brilliant crimson with prominent orange stamens. The leaves are larger near the base and rather succulent.
Flowers most of the year.

Plate 79 Compositae

Fig. 1. **Aster harveyanus** Kuntze (693)
A dainty herb with single flower-heads which may be white, pale pink or mauve with yellow centres. The stem is maroon, and the leaves are lanceolate, rather broad with longitudinal veins. The plant is about 30 cm tall and is found on the higher grassy slopes of the Nyika Plateau.
Flowers October.

Fig. 2. **Erythrocephalum zambesianum** Oliv. & Hiern (114)
Found amongst grass and under trees in most parts of Malawi. It is about 60 cm high, the terminal flower-heads are a deep crimson. The leaves are tough, the undersides covered with a silvery 'down', and the stems with red hairs.
Flowers November to April.

Fig. 3. **Crassocephalum rubens** (Jacq.) S. Moore (176)
The flowers vary in colour from rich blue to purple or pinkish mauve. They are all tubular and are enclosed in a light green involucre with a brown ring of outer bracts. The leaves are alternate and deeply toothed. This is a straggling plant up to 75 cm found throughout the country in grass and scrub.
Flowers February to September.

Fig. 4 **Lactuca lasiorhiza** (O. Hoffm.) C. Jeffrey (730)
An attractive little plant which grows out of hard baked ground, especially after firing. The ray-flowers are pink and squared off at the tips, the centres are yellow. The stems and the leaves, which are bract-like, are maroon and exude a milky sap when broken. Found on Zomba Plateau, Mulanje and Nyika.
Flowers August to October.

Fig. 5 **Athrixia rosmarinifolia** (Sch. Bip. ex Walp.) Oliv. & Hiern (318)
A small plant with slightly woody stems. The leaves are narrow, lanceolate and opposite and wooly underneath. Buds are grey-green with brown calyx tips. The flowers are pink to mauve with yellow centres. It is found on Ndirande, Mulanje and Zomba Plateau and probably on most high ground.
Flowers July to October.

Fig. 6 **Dicoma sessiliflora** Harv. (691)
An erect herb of about 30 cm. The narrow leaves and stem are covered with fine silver 'down'. Flower-heads grow straight off the stem with two or three at the top. The flowers are white and tubular and are enclosed in very prickly, green and white bracts which are longer than the flowers. Although not common it is very widespread in the higher grasslands and woodlands.
Flowers May to October.

Fig. 7 **Dicoma anomala** Sond. subsp. cirsioides (Harv.) Wild (224)
A low trailing plant found falling over rocks and in grass on the Nyika Plateau. The leaves are narrow, alternate and greyish-green. Two or three rather large flower-heads are borne at the tips of the stems. The tubular flowers are brownish pink enclosed in dull red very pointed bracts which turn a lovely shiny straw-colour when dry.
Flowers May to August.

Plate 79   Compositae

Plate 80   Compositae

159

Plate 80   Compositae

Fig. 1. **Gerbera ambigua** (Cass.) Sch. Bip. (430)
The bright yellow flowers are at the top of a 25 cm stalk which is brownish green and covered with fine hairs. The leaves have pink stalks and are bright green above and silvery grey underneath. It grows in marshy ground on the plateaux of Mulanje, Zomba, Nyika and Vipya.
Flowers December to April.

Fig. 2. **Gerbera welwitschii** S. Moore (715)
A neat little plant about 6 cm high. There are two or three yellow terminal flowers, the stems are covered with hairs and the ovate leaves at the base of the plant are green on top and grey underneath. It is found in marshy ground, especially after firing, on Nyika and Zomba Plateaux.
Flowers July and August.

Fig. 3. **Gerbera viridifolia** (DC.) Sch. Bip. (177)
This species is 20-30 cm tall with hairy stems and large ovate leaves with maroon edges. The ray florets are white or very pale pink with darker pink on the outer side. The inner tubular florets are yellow. It is found in open grassland and under Brachystegia on most of the Malawi higher hills and Plateaux.
Flowers May to November.

Fig. 4. **Laggera alata** (D. Don) Sch. Bip. ex Oliv. (277)
Not a very conspicuous herb. It grows to about 75 cm. The bracts turn backwards and the dull pink flowers hang down, never opening fully. The mature fruiting heads forming silvery spheres all over the plant are far more decorative. Common in grassland and woodland.
Flowers June to August.

Fig. 5 **Erlangea sp.** (99)
This is a very attractive little plant about 30 cm tall. The leaves are mainly basal with a few bract-like ones on the branched stem. The flowers are all tubular, the inner ones a deeper purple and shorter than the outer ones. It is found in the open grasslands of the Nyika Plateau.
Flowers December and January.

Fig. 6. **Lactuca calophylla** C. Jeffrey (113)
A very conspicuous plant with its racemes of sulphur-yellow, star-like flowers standing well above the short grasses of the Nyika Plateau. The bracts are grey-green, and the stem is covered with purple hairs. The leaves are nearly all basal, ovate and concave, green above and very heavily veined in purple below. The root is woody and trunk-like. It is fairly common on Nyika and also on the Vipya and Ntchisi Mountain.
Flowers December and January.

BOTANICAL TERMS

Alternate	arranged singly on different sides of a stem.
Anthers	part of the stamen at the top of the filament which contains the pollen.
Arborescent	Attaining to the size and character of a tree.
Axil	The angle between the leaf and the stem.
Axillary	arising from the axil.
Basal	at the base of the plant.
Berry	a juicy fruit with the seeds immersed in pulp.
Bipinnate	when the divisions of a pinnate leaf are themselves pinnate.
Bract	a modified leaf subtending a flower or flower stalk.
Bulb	an underground, swollen stem composed of scaly leaves.
Calyx	outer envelope of a flower; separate or united sepals.
Capsule	a dry dehiscent fruit.
Column	(a) Orchidaceae, the fused stamens and style forming a solid central body. (b) Malvaceae, the filaments joined to form a tube.
Compound	composed of many similar parts as a leaf with many leaflets.
Corm	a kind of solid bulb or tuberous bulb-like root.
Corolla	inner envelope of the flower consisting of free or united petals.
Corona	a circle of appendages between the corolla and stamens, often united into a ring or crown.
Endemic	confined to a region or country and not native anywhere else.
Epicalyx	whorl of bracts below a flower like an extra calyx.
Epiphyte	a plant which grows on another plant or on rocks but which derives nourishment from the air.
Filament	the stalk of a stamen supporting the anther.
Fimbriate	with margins bordered with long slender processes.
Floret	a tiny flower, one of a cluster.
Inferior	of the ovary which is below the corolla and calyx.
Inflorescence	arrangement of flowers on a plant.
Irregular flowers	can be cut into two equal parts in one direction only.
Keel	the two partially united, lowest petals of a papilionaceous flower.
Keeled	ridged along the middle of a flat or convex surface.
Lanceolate	lance-like, long and tapering at the apex.
Leaflet	one part of a compound leaf.
Linear	long and narrow with parallel edges.
Lip	either part of a two lipped flower e.g. Labiatae, longer front petal in flowers such as Disa, Orchidaceae.
Node	the point on the stem at which a leaf or branch is borne.
Obovate	egg-shaped leaf with the broadest part above the middle.
Opposite	of leaves when two are borne at the same node on opposite sides of the stem.
Ovary	that part of the flower which contains the ovules and eventually becomes the fruit.
Ovate	egg-shaped leaf with broadest part below the middle.
Ovule	immature seed in the ovary before fertilization.
Palmate	divided into segments like the palm of a hand.
Parasite	growing on, and getting food from a host plant.
Perianth	floral envelope consisting of calyx or corolla or both.

Petal	part of the corolla, usually brightly coloured.
Pollen	small grains on the anthers containing the male element of the plant.
Pinnate	leaflets arranged on opposite sides of a common stalk.
Procumbent	lying along the ground but not rooting at the nodes.
Raceme	an inflorescence in which the flowers are borne on stalks along an individual stem.
Ray	florets on the margin of a flowerhead of Compositae.
Saprophite	a plant living on decaying vegetable matter.
Sensitive	(of leaves) folding up when touched.
Sepal	a part of the calyx, outer whorl of the perianth.
Sheath	Structure enveloping the base of a leaf or a bud.
Spadix	a flower spike with a fleshy axis eg. Araceae.
Spathe	a large bract enclosing a spadix or two or more bracts enclosing a flower cluster.
Spike	an inflorescence with flowers without stalks along an undivided stem.
Spur	a projection of some part of the flower, usually slender and hollow and often carrying nectar.
Stamen	unit of the flower composed of the filament and anther.
Staminoide	an imperfect stamen, infertile and often looking like a petal.
Standard	the large upper petal of a papilionaceous flower.
Stigma	the part of the style which receives the pollen.
Sterile	non-fertile.
Style	the narrow upper part of the ovary supporting the stigma.
Terrestrial	on or in the ground.
Trifoliate	a compound leaf with three leaflets.
Tuber	thickened underground stem or root acting as a reserve store of nourishment.
Umbel	inflorescence in which the flower stalks spring from the same point. Compound umbel where each ray itself bears an umbel.
Unisexual	having stamens only or ovary, style and stigma only.
Whorl	arrangement of similar parts in a circle at the same level.

Index

	Text Page	Plate No.
Acalypha stuhlmannii	101	51
ACANTHACEAE	84, 85	42, 43
Achyranthes aspera	88	44
Acidanthera aequinoctalis (see Gladiolus callianthus)	17	9
Acrocephalus callianthus	105	53
Aeollanthus njassae	108	54
Aerva leucura	88	44
Aeschynomene abyssinica	136	68
Aeschynomene schimperi	136	68
Aframomum angustifolium	36	18
Agathisanthemum globosum	96	48
Albuca nyikensis	21	11
Albuca sp.	21	11
Alectra sessiflora	80	40
Alepidia longifolia	141	71
Aloe buchananii	28	14
Aloe mawii	28	14
Aloe mzimbana	28	14
AMARANTHACEAE	88	44
Amaranthus hybridus	88	44
AMARYLLIDACEAE	4–8	2–4
Amphicarpa africana	129	65
Androcymbium melanthioides	21	11
Aneilema aequinoctiale	40	20
Aneilema hockii	40	20
Aneilema welwitschii	40	20
Anisopappus lastii	156	78
Anomatheca grandiflora	13	7
Antherotoma naudinii	144	72
ARACEAE	1	1
Argemone mexicana	121	61
Aristea alata	12	6
ASCLEPIADACEAE	89, 92	45, 46
Aster harveyanus	157	79
Astripomoea malvaceae	117	59
Asystasia gangetica	84	42
Athrixia rosmarinifolia	157	79
Azanza garckeana	69	35
Barlaria senensis	85	43
Barlaria spinulosa	85	43
BALSAMINACEAE	93	47
Becium obovatum	109	55
Berkheya zeyheri	156	78
Bidens steppia	156	78
Blaeria kiwuensis	137	69
Blepharis grandis	84	42
Boophone sp.	8	4
BORAGINACEAE	104	52
Borreria dibrachiata	97	49
Brachycorythis pleistophylla	53	27
Brachystelma togoense	92	46
Buchnera hispida	80	40
Buchnera pulchra	80	40
Buchnera similis	80	40
Bulbine abyssinica	21	11
Bulbophyllum oxypterum	56	28
CACTACEAE	101	51
Cadaba kirkii	88	44
CAESALPINIACEAE	116	58
CAMPANULACEAE	73	37
CAPPARACEAE	88	44
CARYOPHYLLACEAE	149	75
Cassia polytricha	116	58
Cephalaria pungens	112	56
Ceratotheca sesamoides	125	63
Ceropegia filipendula	89	45
Ceropegia papillata	89	45
Chironia laxiflora	100	50
Chironia krebsii	100	50
Chlorophytum sp.	24	12
Cleome hirta	88	44
Clematis welwitschii	68	34
Clematopsis scabiosifolia	68	34
Clematopsis uhehensis	68	34
Clerodendrum rotundifolium	140	70
Clerodendrum myricoides	140	70
Clerodendrum c.f. wildii	140	70
Coccinia adoensis	148	74
COMMELINACEAE	37–40	19, 20
Commelina africana	37	19
Commelina aspera	37	19
Commelina diffusa	37	19
Commelina neurophylla	37	19
Commelina zambesiaca	37	19
COMPOSITAE	149–160	75–80
CONVOLVULACEAE	117	59
Costus spectabilis	36	18
Crassocephalum rubens	157	79
Crassula alba	72	36
Crassula argyrophylla	72	36
Crassula globularioides	72	36
CRASSULACEAE	72	36
Craterostigma lanceolatum	76	38
Crinum pedicellatum	4	2
Crocosmia aurea	12	6
Crossandra greenstockii	85	43
Crotalaria laburnifolia	128	64
Crotalaria lachnorphora	128	64
Crotalaria lanceolata	128	64
Crotalaria pallida	128	64
Crotalaria shirensis	128	64
CUCURBITACEAE	148	74
Cyanotis foecunda	40	20
Cyanotis longifolia	40	20
Cyanotis speciosa	40	20
Cycnum adonense	77	39
Cynoglossum geometricum	104	52
Cynorkis kassnerana	53	27
Cynorkis kirkii	53	27
Cyphia sp.	73	37
Cyrtanthus breviflorus	8	4
Cyrtanthus welwitschii	8	4
Dasystachys campanulata	24	12
Datura innoxia	81	41
Delphinium dascycaulon	65	33
Delphinium leroyi	65	33

Index

	Text Page	Plate No.
Delphinium sp.	65	33
Desmodium repandum	136	68
Dicliptera leonotis	84	42
Dicoma anomala	157	79
Dicoma sessiliflora	157	79
Dierama pendulum	17	9
Dietes vegeta	12	6
Dipcadi sp.	29	15
Diplolphium buchananii	141	71
DIPSACACEAE	112	56
Disa concinna	49	25
Disa erubescens	48	24
Disa hamatopetala	49	25
Disa hircicornis	49	25
Disa ornithantha	48	24
Disa robusta	48	24
Disa saxicola	48	24
Disa welwitschii	49	25
DIOSCOREACEAE	116	58
Dioscorea quartiniana	116	58
Disperis dicerochila	53	27
Dissotis canescens	144	72
Dissotis debilis	144	72
Dissotis melleri	144	72
Dissotis senegambiensis	144	72
Dolichos kilimandscharicus	129	65
Drimia zombensis	24	12
Drosera madagascariensis	76	38
DROSERACEAE	76	38
Dyschoriste hildebrantii	85	43
Emilia javanica	156	78
Erica johnstoniana	137	69
ERICACEAE	137	69
ERIOCAULACEAE	33	17
Eriocaulon schimperi	33	17
Eriospermum abyssinicum	29	15
Erlangea sp.	160	80
Erythrocephalum zambesianum	157	79
Eucomis undulata	21	11
Eulophia coeloglossa	41	21
Eulophia complanata	45	23
Eulophia cucullata	44	22
Eulophia euantha	41	21
Eulophia kirkii	45	23
Eulophia livingstoniana	44	22
Eulophia macrantha	45	23
Eulophia orthoplectra	41	21
Eulophia paivaeana	44	22
Eulophia sp.	41	21
Eulophia speciosa	44	22
Eulophia thomsonii	41	21
Eulophia walleri	45	23
Eulophia zeyheri	44	22
Euphorbia depauperata	101	51
Euphorbia hirta	101	51
Euphorbia zambesiana	101	51
EUPHORBIACEAE	101	51
Floscopa glomerata	40	20

	Text Page	Plate No.
Galium stenophyllum	96	48
Gardinia subacaulis	96	48
Geniosporum paludosum	105	53
Genlisea hispidula	76	38
GENTIANACEAE	100	50
GERANIACEAE	112	56
Geranium nyasse	112	56
Geranium vagans	112	56
Gerbera ambigua	160	80
Gerbera viridifolia	160	80
Gerbera welwitschii	160	80
Gererdiina angolensis	80	40
GESNERACEAE	113	57
Gladiolus atropurpureus	16	8
Gladiolus callianthus	17	9
Gladiolus erectiflorus	16	8
Gladiolus laxiflorus	16	8
Gladiolus melleri	16	8
Gladiolus natalensis	16	8
Gloriosa superba	20	10
Gloriosa virescens	20	10
Glossostelma carsonii	92	46
Gnidia buchananii	121	61
Gnidia chrysantha	121	61
Gnidia kraussiana	121	61
Gonotopus boivinii	1	1
GUTTIFERAE	145	73
Habenaria gonatosiphon	52	26
Habenaria macrostele	52	26
Habenaria pubipetala	52	26
Habenaria sp.	52	26
Habenaria tentaculigera	52	26
Habenaria walleri	52	26
Haemanthus multiflorus	5	3
Hebenstretia dentata	124	62
Helichrysum brassii	152	76
Helichrysum flammeiceps	152	76
Helichrysum herbaceum	149	75
Helichrysum lastii	149	75
Helichrysum nitens	152	76
Helichrysum patulifolium	149	75
Helichrysum setosum	149	75
Helichrysum whyteanum	152	76
Hemizygia bracteosa	109	55
Hesperantha petitiana	13	7
Hewittia sublobata	117	59
Hibiscus fuscus	69	35
Hibiscus rhodanthus	69	35
Hybanthus enneaspermus	124	62
Hypericophyllum scabridum	156	78
Hypericum peplidifolium	145	73
Hypericum revolutum	145	73
HYPOXIDACEAE	8	4
Hypoxis dregei	8	4
Hypoxis obtusa	8	4
Impatiens gomphophylla	93	47
Impatiens hochstetteri	93	47
Impatiens richardsiae	93	47

Index

	Text Page	Plate No.		Text Page	Plate No.
Impatiens schulziana	93	**47**	*Moraea sp.*	9	**5**
Indigofera atriceps	132	**66**	*Moraea textilis*	9	**5**
Indigofera dendroides	132	**66**	*Moraea thomsonii*	9	**5**
Inula glomerata	156	**78**	*Mucuna poggei*	133	**67**
Ipomoea alpina	117	**59**	*Mucuna pruriens*	133	**67**
Ipomoea pes-caprae	117	**59**	*Murdannia simplex*	37	**19**
IRIDACEAE	9-17	**5-9**			
Isoglossa grandiflora	84	**42**	*Nervilia sp.*	57	**29**
			Nesaea floribunda	116	**58**
Jasminum meyeri-johannis	145	**73**	*Nicandra physalodes*	81	**41**
Justicia striata	84	**42**	NYMPHAEACEAE	76	**38**
			Nymphaea caerulea	76	**38**
Kaempferia aethiopica	36	**18**			
Kaempferia decora	36	**18**	*Oberonia disticha*	56	**28**
Kaempferia rhodesica	36	**18**	OCHNACEAE	137	**69**
Kaempferia rosea	36	**18**	*Ochna macrocalyx*	137	**69**
Kalanchoe lanceolata	72	**36**	OLEACEA	145	**73**
Kniphofia grantii	25	**13**	ONAGRACEAE	137	**69**
Kniphofia linearifolia	25	**13**	ORCHIDACEAE	41-60	**21-30**
Kniphofia sp.	25	**13**	*Orthosiphon allenii*	109	**55**
Kniphofia splendida	25	**13**	*Orthosiphon rubicundus*	109	**55**
Knowltonia transvaalensis	68	**34**	OROBANCHACEAE	76	**38**
Kohautia coccinea	97	**49**	*Orobanche minor*	76	**38**
Kohautia cuspidata	96	**48**	*Osteospermum monocephalum*	156	**78**
			Otomeria elatior	97	**49**
LABIATAE	105-109	**53-55**	OXALIDACEAE	125	**63**
Lactuca calophylla	160	**80**	*Oxalis chapmaniae*	125	**63**
Lactuca lasiorhiza	157	**79**	*Oxalis corniuculata*	125	**63**
Lageneria sphaerica	148	**74**			
Laggera alata	160	**80**	*Pachycarpus lineolatus*	92	**46**
Lantana camara	140	**70**	PAPAVERACEAE	121	**61**
Lapeirousia erythrantha	13	**7**	PAPILIONACEAE	128-136	**64-68**
Lapeirousia grandifolia			*Parochetus communis*	129	**65**
(see *Anomatheca grandiflora*)	13	**7**	*Pavonia columella*	69	**35**
LENTIBULARIACEAE	76	**38**	*Pavonia patens*	69	**35**
Leonotis decadonta	108	**54**	*Pavonia urens*	69	**35**
Leucas nyassae	108	**54**	PEDALIACEAE	125	**63**
Lightfootia glomerata	73	**37**	*Pelagonium luridum*	112	**56**
LILIACEAE	20-32	**10-16**	*Pentanisia schweinfurthii*	97	**49**
Liparis neglecta	57	**29**	*Pentas geophila*	97	**49**
Liparis nervosa	57	**29**	*Pentas longiflora*	97	**49**
Lippia javanica	140	**70**	*Physalis peruviana*	81	**41**
Lobelia blantyrensis	73	**37**	*Pimpinella huillensis*	141	**71**
Lobelia intertexta	73	**37**	*Platycoryne crocea*	57	**29**
Lobelia mildbraedii	73	**37**	*Platycoryne mediocris*	57	**29**
LORANTHACEAE	64	**32**	*Polycarpaea eriantha*	149	**75**
Loranthus albizziae	64	**32**	*Polygala albida*	120	**60**
Loranthus blantyrianus	64	**32**	*Polygala macrostigma*	120	**60**
Loranthus curviflorus	64	**32**	*Polygala petitiana*	120	**60**
Ludwigia octovalvis	137	**69**	*Polygala virgata var. decora*	120	**60**
LYTHRACEAE	116	**58**	POLYGALACEAE	120	**60**
			POLYGONACEAE	88	**44**
Macrostyloma axillare	129	**65**	*Polygonum strigosum*	88	**44**
MALVACEAE	69	**35**	*Polystachya johnstonii*	56	**28**
Margaretta rosea	92	**46**	*Polystachya s.p.*	56	**28**
MELASTOMATACEAE	144	**72**	PROTEACEAE	61	**31**
Momordica foetida	148	**74**	*Protea angolensis*	61	**31**
Monopsis stellarioides	73	**37**	*Pycnostachys stuhlmanni*	105	**53**
Moraea angusta	12	**6**	*Pycnostachys urticifolia*	105	**53**
Moraea schimperi	9	**5**	(and variant)	105	**53**

165

Index

	Text Page	Plate No.
Radinosiphon leptostachya	13	7
RANUNCULACEAE	65–68	33–34
Ranunculus raeae	68	34
Rhamphicarpa tubulosa	77	39
Rhipsalis baccifera	101	51
Romulea campanuloides	17	9
ROSACEAE	145	73
RUBIACEAE	96–97	48–49
Rubus ellipticus	145	73
Ruellia prostrata sensu	84	42
Salvia coccina	109	55
Satyrium anomalum	60	30
Satyrium atherstonei	60	30
Satyrium breve	60	30
Satyrium buchananii	60	30
Satyrium neglectum	60	30
Scabiosa austro-africana	112	56
Schwartzkopffia lastii	56	28
Scilla buchananii	32	16
Scilla cordifolia	29	15
Scilla natalensis	32	16
Scilla rigidifolia	29	15
SCROPHULARIACEAE	76–80	38–40
Scutellaria paucifolia	105	53
Sebaea grandis	100	50
Sebaea longicaulis	100	50
SELAGINACEAE	124	62
Selago thomsonii var thomsonii	124	62
Selago thyrsoidea	124	62
Sesamum angolense	125	63
SOLANACEAE	81	41
Solanum panduriforme	81	41
Sopubia ramosa	80	40
Sparrmannia ricinocarpa	116	58
Sphenostylis marginata	138	68
Sphenostylis stenocarpa	129	65
Stathmostelma pauciflorum	89	45
Stathmostelma spectabile	89	45
Stenoglottis fimbriata	53	27
Streptocarpus buchananii	113	57
Streptocarpus erubescens	113	57
Streptocarpus goetzei	113	57
Striga asiatica	77	39
Striga gesnerioides	77	39
Striga pubiflora	77	39
Swertia johnsonii	100	50

	Text Page	Plate No.
TECOPHILAEACEAE	33	17
Tephrosia nyikensis	132	66
Thunbergia kirkiana	85	43
Thunbergia lancifolia	85	43
THYMELAEACEAE	121	61
TILIACEAE	116	58
Trachyandra saltii	24	12
Trachycalymma cristatum	89	45
Trichodesma hockii	104	52
Trichodesma physaloides	104	52
Trichodesma zeylanicum	104	52
Trifolium simense	132	66
Tritonia laxifolia	12	6
Trochomeria macrocarpa	148	74
Tulbaghia cameronii	24	12
TURNERACEAE	116	58
UMBELLIFERAE	141	71
Utricularia livida	76	38
Utricularia reflexa	76	38
VELLOZIACEAE	33	17
Vellozia sp. (see Xerophyta)	33	17
VERBENACEAE	140	70
Vernonia adoensis	153	77
Vernonia chloropappa	153	77
Vernonia gerberiformis	153	77
Vernonia petersii	153	77
Vernonia poskeana	153	77
Vernonia superba	153	77
Vigna pygmaea	129	65
Vigna vexillata	132	66
Viola abyssinica	124	62
VIOLACEAE	124	62
Wahlenbergia virgata	73	37
Walleria mackenzii	33	17
Wormskoldia longipedunculata	116	58
Wurmbea tenuis	32	16
Xerophyta sp.	33	17
ZINGERBERACEAE	36	18